MIGHTY MAN OF VALOR

BY W. Phillip Keller

Africa's Wild Glory
Canada's Wild Glory
Splendour From the Land
Splendour From the Sea
Under Wilderness Skies
Under Desert Skies
As a Tree Grows
Bold Under God—Charles Bowen
A Shepherd Looks at Psalm 23
A Layman Looks at the Lord's Prayer
Rabboni . . . Which Is to Say, Master
A Shepherd Looks at the Good Shepherd and His Sheep
Taming Tension
Expendable
Mountain Splendor
Mighty Man of Valor

MIGHTY MAN OF VALOR

Gideon:
The Sword of the Lord

W. Phillip Keller

Fleming H. Revell Company
Old Tappan, New Jersey

All royalties from the sale of this book go to The Gideons International of Canada for distribution of the Scriptures worldwide.

Library of Congress Cataloging in Publication Data

Keller, Weldon Phillip, date
   Mighty man of valor.

    1. Gideon, judge of Israel—Fiction. I. Title.
PZ4.K2793Mi 1979 [PR9199.3.K4145]   813'.5'4
ISBN 0-8007-0997-7   78-26975

TO
My friends, the Gideons

Contents

Preface

THIS BOOK is a brief, biographical study of a rather remarkable man. He emerges out of the gloom of ancient Israel's history like a comet blazing across the night sky. For a few short years—about forty—his life and character dominate the darkness of the times. Then with his passing, once more his people sink into despondency and despair.

The narrative of Gideon's triumph under God stirs our spirits and thrills our souls. Here we see what the Lord can achieve with a person who is available to Him. The exploits recounted and triumphs attained against incredible odds weave a tapestry of bright design that can enliven our understanding of what it means for a man to come under God's command.

Gideon is given to us as an example of God's dealing with the plastic, moldable material of our common humanity. We can readily identify with the strengths and weaknesses of his character. We can relate to his inhibitions as a human being. We can also discover some of the secrets to greatness under God's good hand.

Beyond this there is a rather remarkable parallel between this period in Israel's story and our own twentieth century. The increasing sense of despair, the gathering gloom, the apprehension of evil—all are here. Yet amid this period, as in Gideon's time, God looks for gallant men who will respond to His call. Perhaps you the reader will become a modern Gideon.

Acknowledgments

THE ENTHUSIASM of the men and women with whom I first shared these Bible studies has been an inspiration. It was a joy to see their interest in God's Word as we explored Gideon's life together.

It was thoughtful of Mr. Dave Lacey to tape all these sessions. He put this material at my disposal for assistance in preparation of the manuscript.

My wife, Ursula, has been so faithful in typing the book, correcting my spelling, and making helpful suggestions along the way.

The immediate and hearty cooperation of Fleming H. Revell Company, and especially their editor Mr. Ernie Owen, in producing the book has been a happy encouragement.

Above all I am deeply grateful to God for the enormous joy and enthusiasm given to me personally in my study of Gideon's life. It has been like a prospector who came across a rich vein of pure gold buried beneath the overburden of accumulated centuries.

To all, my hearty thanks and genuine gratitude!

MIGHTY MAN OF VALOR

1

Driven Underground

IT WAS 1256 B.C., roughly two hundred years since those titanic times when Joshua and his cohorts had stormed into Jericho. Its walls flattened beneath the trumpet blasts of Israel's forces, Jericho was the first enemy bastion in Canaan to fall. Under the guidance of God, Joshua's armies had swept across most of Palestine, the so-called Promised Land, taking territory and establishing power over the Canaanite occupants.

Those were heady days. Victory was in the air. Jehovah God, the Lord of Israel, was leading His special people to great power and prominence. He was their God, their King, their Governor, and their Commander. Under Him their theocracy flourished.

But the ensuing two hundred years had seen a terrible turnaround. In direct contravention of God's explicit commands, this stubborn, strong-willed, stiff-necked nation refused to eject all of the pagan peoples of Palestine. They had permitted small pockets of the local populace to remain scattered among them. Like a virulent disease

temporarily suppressed, they would later erupt to con-
taminate and infect all of Israel with their false ideologies
and corrupt customs.

Again and again, Israel, as a nation, had been alerted to
the awful peril of compromising with the Canaanite tribes
(sometimes referred to collectively as the Amorites). The
Lord Jehovah who had brought this nation out of serfdom
in Egypt by such a spectacular exodus, was keenly desir-
ous to have their undivided allegiance. Yet, instead, they
had allowed themselves to be subverted by the insidious
fifth column remaining in their country. By degrees they
had turned from the true and living God to pursue the
pagan rites of Baal, Ashtaroth, and other despicable
deities.

This chosen people of God, called to be a select society,
had become contaminated by the obscene culture of their
contemporary world. The repulsive rites of spurious reli-
gions were followed with fervor. Temple prostitution,
both male and female; homosexuality; unbridled licentiousness; passionate preoccupation with sexual perver-
sion; greed; avarice; and illicit gain were the overwhelming drives that engulfed a society sinking into de-
bauchery.

It was an appalling performance played out upon the
pathetic stage of Palestine. The whole of the then-known
world looked on askance. The neighboring nations and
nomadic tribes surrounding Canaan were both bemused
and baffled by Israel's behavior. God Himself was deeply
grieved.

This special people of such noble promise, instead of
achieving greatness, had groveled in the grime and ignominy of their contemporaries. To use scriptural language, they had forgotten and forsaken the true and living

God to follow false gods. They had rejected and repudiated the Lord Jehovah who had delivered them from
their ancient oppressors. They had sinned in seeking only
their own selfish interests as opposed to complying with
the explicit commands of a righteous Ruler who had only
their own best interests in mind.

The net result had been catastrophe upon catastrophe
for Israel. Precisely as it had been predicted and prophe-
sied by her leaders, this people would willfully sow the
windblown seeds of sin, later to reap a hurricane
whirlwind of disaster.

Again and again, they would be pillaged and plundered
by the powerful nations around them. They would be
caught up and tossed about like chaff in the winds of war.
The fierce raiders of Mesopotamia, Moab, Canaan, and
Philistia would all have their heyday planting their cruel
warrior heels on the stubborn necks of this stiff-necked
nation.

Israel was to suffer enormous losses. She was trampled
into subjection. Her people were driven into black despair. Hope was gone. Fear and foreboding gripped their
hearts.

Out of the depths of their despondency, they would cry
again to God. Once more their impossible plight would
point them back to the place of deliverance. Again, they
would repent and recant of their perverse and appalling
folly. In earnest entreaty they would implore Jehovah to
redeem them from their predicament.

And He did!

Like wave following wave to break upon the beach of
time, so the story of Israel, for two hundred tormenting
years, had been *sinning-suffering-salvation*, then again
sinning-suffering-salvation. Only a most gracious, gener-

ous, and magnanimous God could or would put up with such a story.

In His compassion and concern for His own chosen people, He provided them with a whole series of outstanding individuals who came forward, some as judges, to deliver Israel from her recurring dilemmas. There had been Othniel, Ehud, Shamgar, Deborah, and Barak.

But in spite of all these, Israel, like a sow returning to wallow in the mud, had turned again to revel in wickedness. So for seven long grinding years, God had allowed the Midianites, fierce desert nomads from the Arab wastes, to devastate the Israelites. Cruel, wild, and ruthless—these warrior people raided relentlessly. They swept in from east of the Jordan, a veritable desert storm of destruction. As prolific as the desert locusts, they came in hordes, mounted on camels, bringing with them their families, flocks, and armed forces. Their invasion was so massive, so overmastering, so maliciously unmerciful that Israel was driven underground.

It is worthy of note that Scripture makes it abundantly clear, the repeated devastation of Israel was *not* something contrived by the devil, but rather actually arranged by God. It was the operation of the eternal divine principle of reaping what one plants.

These were still God's people, in the place of His own appointment, under His paternal care. And if they simply insisted on being deliberately disobedient, they would have to undergo corrective discipline. There is nothing malicious or vindictive in this action on God's part. For whom He loves, He chastens. And we do Him enormous injustice to think or suggest that the suffering endured by His people was merely a means to indulge His pique.

This is a ploy perpetrated by His enemies, but it has no

place or part in our thinking as His people. He always permits punishment in order to achieve optimum benefits in the best interests of His people. To do otherwise would be to betray Himself and those in His care.

At this point in Israel's story, so oppressive were the Midianites that their victims were literally living underground to survive. They had holed up in caves, dens, and underground strongholds. To show oneself brazenly could easily mean immediate liquidation. It was a brutal business that made men into moles. Perhaps at no other time in all of her history had Israel lived at such a humbled level.

A man dare not declare himself. Whatever he did must be done under cover in secret. Fear and foreboding for the future filled mens' minds and shriveled their spirits. Life was grim and gaunt. There was no gaiety. If grain was planted or grapes were gathered, no one knew if they would ever taste the loaf or drink the vintage. Hope was dead. Morale was low. All the nation was bankrupt— emotionally, spiritually, economically.

The Midianites were a motley mob. Sons of the desert sands, they were distant descendents of Abraham, just as the Israelites were. Their federal forefather had been Ishmael, ill-begotten son of Hagar, sired by Abraham in an abortive attempt to shortcut God's great promise to provide him with posterity. Israel, on the other hand had sprung from Isaac, Sarah's son, begotten in her old age by a miraculous conception in accord with the commitments of God to His friend Abraham.

Here, some 650 years later, the offspring of one son was being used as a scourge to correct the progeny of the other. The long-term consequences of a man's actions are enormous. And even to this day, in our late twentieth century, the ongoing consequences of Abraham's ill-advised action are with us. The enduring alienation of the Arab and Israeli nations stands as a solemn reminder that no man is an island who lives alone to himself. Whatever we do touches a thousand other lives and bears directly upon uncounted other careers.

Like great massive swarms of locusts, the Midianites moved relentlessly across Palestine. Being the first people to domesticate the desert camel, they enjoyed enormous advantage in military mobility. Their hooved hordes roamed and raided relentlessly from the eastern outposts of the Transjordan to the Mediterranean littoral. No corner of the country escaped their rapacious ruin.

Proud, arrogant, hawklike warriors, they gloated in their fierce freedom. Their sharp swords and shining spears were notoriously vicious. They drew blood with a grin, took slaves with impunity, and left behind a landscape reddened with blood and blackened by fire.

Beneath their brutal, cruel oppression, Israel lay crushed and mangled. It was a broken, beaten, helpless people who once again recalled forlornly the glory of their God and cried to Him for help.

2

Then–Gideon

THE CRY FOR HELP which went up from Israel was not unheard. It was a cry of desperation from a people driven underground. It was a cry of despair from a nation in bankruptcy. It was a cry of helplessness to the Lord of heaven who alone could lift them out of their horrible pit of distress. Only He could rescue them from the miry clay of their calamities trampled beneath the fierce feet of their foes.

As with Israel, so with most of us. It often takes a long struggle of self-assertion before we lie prostrate and helpless. The pride of our personalities and the steellike perverseness of our wills prevent us from turning to God for assistance. The pugnaciousness of our makeup is such that not until we are virtually knocked down and laid out prostrate do the bleary eyes of our dull spiritual understanding turn longingly to Him who is the source of our help.

Yet, wonder of wonders, it is precisely at this point that God is there, watching, waiting, willing to reach out to men in the depths of their need. This was true for Israel, a beaten and bedraggled people literally buried from view in their dens, caves, and underground hideouts.

The divine response to their prayers was not immediate deliverance or an instantaneous miracle. It was a message. It was a statement from God as to the cause of their calamity. They simply had "to see" the reason for their dilemma. So a prophet, a "seer," a man with a word from the Lord, was sent to this stubborn nation to make it see why it was in such straits.

Patiently but pointedly they were reminded that it was their God Jehovah who had brought them out of the bondage and slavery in Egypt. It was He who had rescued them from the heavy hand of their slave masters. It was He who had led them and their little ones through the wilderness. It was He who had brought them in triumph into the land of promise. It was He who had driven out their foes before them. It was He who had bestowed upon them this land flowing with milk and honey—a land rich with resources of fertile valleys, running streams, lovely forests, and lush grasslands. It was He who had asked only for their loyal allegiance and gentle obedience in return for all the benefits bestowed by His generous hand.

But Israel, like strong-willed, wayward children, had quickly forgotten all of that. In their self-indulgent pride, they had deliberately disdained His directions to keep themselves from the pollution of the pagan people around them. Boldly and with bald-faced abandon, they had turned from Him to follow the false gods of their ancient foes. It was a foolhardy course of self-destruction on which they had set their souls. And the ultimate end of their adamant disobedience was their present peril.

There is a way which seemeth right unto a man, but the end thereof are the ways of death.

Proverbs 14:12

The voice of the living God had been ignored. The commandments intended to preserve them as a people in peace and prosperity had been spurned. The edicts given to lift them to lofty, noble living on a level far above their contemporaries had been scorned.

The net result was not just that they had broken God's laws, but rather, even more terrifying, was the simple fact that those divine laws—unchangeable principles—had broken them as a people. It is impossible to spurn the laws of the Lord and not suffer appalling consequences. In mercy, understanding, and goodwill, they have been designed in divine love for the well-being of men.

Transgress them, and they will ultimately pulverize you.

Disregard them, and they will eventually destroy you.

Break them blatantly, and they will break you.

Fortunately for us it is the person and people broken in heart and contrite in spirit to whom the Lord draws near. Even in the apparent harshness of divine discipline there lies the enduring care of a compassionate Saviour who comes at the cry of His suffering ones.

This is ever the profound and poignant picture of God's dealing with difficult people. Whether it be one person or an entire nation, His response to our pleas and His concern for our plight is that of the Father for His children.

This poor man cried, and the Lord heard him, and saved him out of all his troubles.

Psalms 34:6

O the incredible generosity of such a gracious God. He is the Helper of the helpless. And it is the prayer of the helpless which is never left unanswered. In total weakness their lies the vacuum of utter need into which God moves with enormous alacrity and strength.

So one day, in the sparse shade of a shriveled, dusty oak, an angel sat watching a young man doing a most peculiar thing. He was a strong, virile young man, of perhaps thirty years, a father, who seemed very afraid and acted furtively. He had climbed down into the bottom of a deep, shadowed winepress. There, hidden from public view, Gideon was threshing out a small bundle of wheat.

It was a dusty, throat-choking task in such cramped quarters. Normally grain was threshed out on an open floor where the passing breezes could carry away the dust and chaff. But if Gideon was to have bread at all to feed his young family, it would have to be found in this very difficult devious manner. To display what he was doing openly would have invited a raid from some hawk-eyed Midian marauders.

Gideon's home village was Ophrah, meaning "dustiness" or "the dusty place." It was not the most promising setting, but it was where his father Joash and his forefathers before him had homesteaded in the more desolate region of Manasseh, an arid area of northeast Palestine.

For a while the divine visitor watched the young man sweating at his work. It was hot, stuffy, and cramped where he beat out the wheat. Every once in a while Gideon would straighten his back, lift his head, and glance around furtively to make sure no one had seen him. Then suddenly his eyes met those of the visitor, and the angel spoke.

His first words were strange, almost filled with satire. "The Lord is with thee, thou mighty man of valor."

Both statements seemed absurd. First of all, where was the God of Israel? Where was this One, whom all his young life Gideon had been told had done such great exploits for His people? Where was this miracle worker who had permitted Israel to fall prey to the ruinous raids of the Midianites?

Second, anyone with eyes to see could know that he was no mighty man of valor. Gallant generals and fearless warriors did not hide from the enemy in winepresses. They did not beat out a bit of grain in secret shame.

The angel was no passing apparition. He was not just the fleeting fantasy of this man's imagination. He was more than the figment of daydreams.

He was the living presence of the living Lord. He was the person of whom it was said in Isaiah 63:8, 9: "Surely they are my people, children that will not lie: so he was their Saviour. In all their affliction he was afflicted, *and the angel of his presence saved them:* in his love and in his pity he redeemed them; and he bare them, and carried them all the days of old" (italics added).

This is the One of whom Joash, his father, had so often told Gideon the heart-thumping tales of old. Joash had brought up Gideon to reverence God. Often as they sat gently in the cool shade of the sturdy old oak, the gray-haired gentleman had regaled his son with the ancient exploits of Jehovah in bringing Israel out of bondage into freedom. In fact, his name *Joash* meant just that, "Jehovah, God, has helped."

But for the last seven terrible years, such tales had seemed but empty stories that mocked a man and shriveled his soul. There had been no sign of a saving God in their land. Instead only the hated, clanking camel caravans of the cruel Midianites. Mercilessly they had plundered and pillaged the villages and fields of his people. Only poverty, ruin, and suffering remained.

"Gideon, the Lord is with you!" Surely that was a shock. If he had been a less respectful young man, he might well have laughed back in cynical disdain. Yet somehow, deep within his shriveled spirit, the youthful farmer felt sure this was the Lord, the Saviour of His people.

But how could he be sure? How could he know beyond the least small shadow of doubt?

"Surely," he protested, rubbing the dust out of his bloodshot eyes, and brushing the chaff from his long black locks. "Surely, Jehovah has forsaken His people. This is self-evident. If not, then how come Israel is ground down under the hard hooves of the Midianite hordes?"

Perhaps in his plight, anger, and dismay Gideon had forgotten the pointed message of God's prophet. He had failed to fully realize that Israel's disobedience had led ultimately to this disaster.

Down in his winepress he indulged in grievous self-pity. It just had to be God's fault. It was Jehovah who had forsaken His chosen ones. It was the Lord who had bungled things a bit. It was His mismanagement that had allowed the Midianites to grind Israel into the ground.

Self-pity of this sort is the most insidious of sins. It is probably the most diabolical insult any of us can hurl at God. It implies that He cannot be trusted to handle our affairs nor direct our lives. It implies that He is quite incompetent to care for us as His own. Yet it is a habit many of us indulge in frequently with utter impunity. Only a generous, gracious God could endure such insults from self-centered men.

Happily for Gideon, the Lord did not retaliate against

this diatribe. He did not lash out at the young man's insolent remarks. He did not rake him across the coals of a guilty conscience for his cynicism. Rather He redirected his attention and focused it on a challenge greater than anything Gideon had ever seen or known. He lifted the young man's gaze from a handful of grain to a gigantic conquest of the enemy—to the salvation of his nation.

"Gideon, go!" It was a dynamic command, a divine imperative! "Gideon, I am here; the Lord God of Israel is with you . . . I am present to preserve and empower you . . . this is your strength, this is your power, this is your energizing force . . . in short, this is your might. Go in the strength of the Lord and save Israel from the Midianites. I am sending you!"

This was heady stuff. This was as exciting as the trumpet blasts that flattened the walls of Jericho. This was a clarion call to action. This was a challenge to stir the blood and quicken the pulse.

For just a moment or two Gideon's vision moved from a meager bundle of unthreshed wheat lying at his dusty feet. It shifted from the barren, blasted fields around his father's village. It lifted from the clanking chains of the hated and feared camel trains of Midian. Briefly, brightly, Gideon felt sure he could fell ten thousand of the foe.

Gideon—yes, he, Gideon, had been named "the cutter down," "the overcomer." Perhaps it was not just a jest after all. Perhaps this visitor might just have a point. Mayhap in God's hand he might yet become another of the great heroes in Israel's history.

But how?

Uneasily he shifted from one foot to the other. He brushed the clinging wheat chaff from his bare sweaty shoulders. He rubbed the dust from his strong, brawny arms browned by the summer sun.

His mind flashed back briefly to the angel's first remarks in his salutation. "Thou mighty man of valor! You gallant general!" Somehow he sensed deep down within himself that this was half truth, half fiction. He knew all too well his own fears, his own inhibitions, his own misgivings, his own inherent apprehension and foreboding.

Yet beyond this, those stirring words had given him a dazzling, daring vision of what he might become—"a mighty man of valor"—under God's great hand.

This initial encounter with the Lord, this personal contact with his God, redirected the whole thrust of Gideon's life. He would never be the same again. His life had been touched from above.

Fortunately for him and for his nation—yes for all of us—God saw in Gideon much more than just a young farmer. He saw more than just another discouraged man on the land. He saw locked up in this life all the potential of a gallant general.

Just as Jacob, "the deceiver," became Israel, a prince with God; just as Simon, "the unstable one," became Peter, a rock; just as Saul "the persecutor of God's people," became Paul, champion of the church, so God can take any one of us, if we will allow Him, and transform us into giants of faith under His good hand.

3

Gideon's Conversion

THE STIMULATING CHALLENGE set before Gideon to deliver his nation from the tyranny of the desert nomads fired his spirit. It inflamed his enthusiasm. It made his mind race madly.

"But how?" It was one thing to envisage great dreams and conquests. It was quite another to carry them out. His aspirations might well be enormous but how could they ever be achieved with such meager and paltry resources? The angel had spoken rather grandly about saving all Israel from her foes. Yet here he was, only a simple countryman without wealth, prestige, or power to carry out the command of God.

Like most of us when given a job to do for the Lord, he began to dredge up a score of excuses why it could not be done. "After all," Gideon protested feebly, "my family is poor!" They had always been tillers of the soil and the arid, rocky ground of their northern region of Manasseh at best was only marginal land. What was more, his tribe was by no means a mighty military force in Israel the way

29

both Ephraim and Judah had been. "To top it all off, I am the youngest and least important member of my father's family," he explained painfully, as he shuffled his bare feet in the powdery, dusty soil beneath the oak. "So really, what can I do?"

There was no great merit in such a declaration. It did not necessarily imply any special humility. Rather it was a simple, straightforward statement of his limitations and position.

Any man, however, who is to achieve great exploits for God, simply has to get beyond this point. He must see that it has to be the resources from a source greater than himself which will achieve the desired end. He has to depend, not on his own human ingenuity, but on divine intervention, for success.

The threefold strands interwoven into true humility are: first, a recognition that each of us has in fact been given certain gifts from above; second, that if placed at God's disposal, they can be used to achieve remarkable results; third, giving the Lord genuine, open credit for both their bestowal and their effectiveness in His hands. To people of this spirit, God delights to draw near.

So the prompt response made to Gideon was the eternal, enduring commitment the Lord always makes to us: "I will be with you!" It sounds so simple. Yet, if taken sincerely, it is so terribly important. The whole of our life pivots on this point. It is the divine diamond on which the compass needle of our will balances with precision. "God is with His people. God is among His own. More than this, God's very person, presence, and power indwells, permeates, and energizes us." It is imperative both to see and move on this premise.

As Paul put it so pointedly in writing to his friends at

Philippi: "It is God which worketh in you both to will and to do of his good pleasure" (Philippians 2:13).

It was in this power that Gideon would pulverize the Midianites. Their hosts would fall before him like a single soldier smitten in combat. One man with God was a majority no matter how overwhelming the odds were arrayed against him. This was not just fanciful theory or theology; it was to be demonstrated in the grim field of battle.

But Gideon was still far from sure this could be so. He wanted verification that he was not embarking on some foolhardy escapade of his own imagination. A son of the soil, he needed to have some solid evidence that this was God's initiative and enterprise. He was not a man to chase the clouds. He wanted concrete confirmation that it was God, very God, who was calling him into action. He demanded definite reassurance that this was no will-o'-the-wisp daydream.

To his great credit Gideon was big enough and generous enough to pay for such proof out of his own pocket. It is a measure of the man that he did not ask the Lord to do everything. He was prepared to play his part in the enterprise even at great personal expense.

He invited his guest of honor to wait patiently in the shade of the old oak tree while he prepared him a princely meal. The ingredients for this banquet were not easy to come by. The enemy raiders had stripped Israel so mercilessly that scarcely a sheep, ox, or donkey remained. Yet, somehow, a few stray goats must have been overlooked by the marauders. And out of these Gideon had managed to spare a kid, hidden perhaps in the back of a cave, where it escaped the sharp eyes of the Midianites.

He excused himself from his royal visitor and went into

his humble home to prepare the meal. The kid, which otherwise would have fed his own family, was butchered and boiled in its own rich pungent broth. Taking the small basket of grain he had just beaten out in the wine-press, he proceeded to grind it into flour and bake it into sweet, fresh unleavened cakes that crunched crisply between a man's teeth.

This was the fare that otherwise would have sustained him and his family during their famine days. It had all been saved and conserved with enormous care and diligence. Food was scarce, rare, and terribly valuable. Every handful of meal spelled one more day of survival. Every fragment of meat meant another few hours of strength to endure the torture and tyranny of these tough times. Bread was more precious than silver. Meat was more valuable than gold. Together, meat, bread, and broth spelled life itself.

The angel assured Gideon he would be glad to linger there. He did not despise the generosity of His humble host. This meal prepared in His honor spoke louder than ten thousand words. It was a genuine gesture of self-sacrifice that surpassed any protestations of loyalty Gideon may have made with his lips.

Sacrifice of this sort is something that springs from the depths of love. It is love in action. For to love is to lose one's self; to give one's self away with abandon; to share with no thought of return or recompense. It is to care enough to give and give at great personal cost. The price of true sacrifice is very severe and very stern.

Sacrifice never comes out of our surplus. It comes only out of the very cost of our own survival.

And for this God is always willing and ready to wait.

In fact He has been waiting for such sacrifice for a long,

long time. Down across the long painful centuries of human history, He has found only a few who are prepared to go this far in making themselves totally available to Himself and His purposes on the planet. The reason being the enormous personal cost involved from which most of us recoil.

This momentous day the Lord waited quietly, seated on one of the great gray boulders beneath the scrubby desert oak. There was nothing spectacular or dramatic about the setting. Perhaps a vulture wheeled in the hot sky, drawn by the blood and offal of the slaughtered kid. Flies buzzed over the remains of the skeleton. The thorn brush crackled in the fire where Gideon prepared his peasant meal. Little streams of perspiration trickled across his tanned face.

At last all was ready. The young man emerged from back of his humble little house to serve his guest. In his eyes there shone the commingled light of love and respect. He was bringing the best he had—in one hand a basket of boiled meat, in the other a bowl of rich dark gravy. Together with the crisp, fresh-baked bread they comprised a banquet fit for royalty.

Standing silently, unmoving, before the angel, Gideon extended his gifts to Him. It was an electric moment. A man before his God. A man alone with his Lord. A man laying what he had on the line. He did not need to speak. This was not the time for explanations or discussion or even dialogue. It was the instant of intense and intimate encounter. At this point the "true" Gideon met the true God. And in that instant not only was God touched, but also the man was touched. He would never be the same again.

The visitor did not partake of the repast prepared with

such painstaking care. He did not take it lightly.

Instead, He instructed the young countryman to lay it all out on a rock nearby. Would it be wasted? Would the bread, meat, and gravy be swarmed over with flies and snatched away by the vultures?

Gideon did not protest. He raised no objections. Apparently he was not even piqued by his guest's unwillingness to take the present. It seemed strange, but he was beyond asking questions. He simply did as he was instructed.

Gently he laid the little loaves of unleavened bread on the great gray granite rock. He placed the pieces of steaming, fragrant flesh beside the bread. Then, taking the broth, he poured it over the whole until it ran down the rock in little rivulets of rich, pungent sweetness.

Not even the gravy was kept for himself!

This was no easy thing for a man whose family was famished and whose own lips scarcely ever touched such a meal these dark days. It was no easy thing to see the nourishing, life-sustaining food laid out on a rock when it might be lying in his stomach, now pinched and gaunt with hunger pains. It was no easy thing to see what might otherwise spell strength for him, literally spilled out upon the ground.

God's ways simply are not our ways.

His methods are not men's methods.

His estimate of things is diametrically different from ours.

To Gideon this may have seemed an enormous loss.

To God it represented an enormous gain.

For in his giving, Gideon had shown his total availability to God. Whatever he possessed was now at God's disposal. More than that, he had demonstrated his willingness to let go of anything in his hand in order to put it in God's keeping.

This was a profound principle proven by this quiet gesture of implicit obedience. Not until we let go of what we own does it become God's to do with as He chooses. We may claim that all we have is His. But only when it is laid out freely from an open, ungrasping hand does He ever take it from us.

God does not wrestle away our resources from us. He does not uncurl our fingers from their grasping, tight clutch upon our possessions. He waits, instead, for our hand to be opened by a generous, honest heart.

The angelic visitor, responding to Gideon's prompt and ready obedience, reached out to touch the sacrifice. At once celestial fire flamed from the rock consuming the bread and flesh in flames. Then the Lord vanished from view.

But it was enough!

Gideon had been honored with the sign he sought.

It was the Lord God of his people who had met with him.

What he had offered had been accepted.

What he had given had been taken.

What he had done had been approved.

If a man will lose his life for the Lord, he will find it. Gideon had given what he had. He had gotten God in return. He had turned over what he owned to God, and God had reached out to touch and take it to Himself. He would never be quite the same Gideon again. He had crossed the "great divide." There was now no going back to his former life-style. He was a man chosen, called, and appointed to signal service.

We often are inclined to look around ourselves and see

certain men or women whom God appears to use in unusual ways. Their lives have a certain incandescence
about them which ignites others they touch. We wonder
why. We ask: "How is it their characters and careers seem
to count so heavily for Christ?"

The answer, more often than not, is a fairly simple one.
These are invariably people who have sacrificed themselves for the Saviour. It costs something very dear to do
this. It involves much more than mere lip service in which
we claim to have laid all on the altar of sacrifice while
clinging tenaciously to our tiny hoarded resources. As
David of old declared so vehemently, there must be a
different view: "I will not offer unto the Lord a sacrifice
that costs me nothing!"

For if we do, it is not a sacrifice at all, but an insult.

It is the person prepared to pay the price of genuine,
personal privation who will see God.

This happened to Gideon. He cried out in wonderment,
"O Lord God! I have seen the angel of the Lord, face-to-
face."

As ever of old, this is not cause for alarm or dismay.
God always comes to us in gracious goodwill and reassuring peace. He confirms to our spirits the gentle strength of
His presence. Fear is dispelled, and our anxious hearts are
stilled by the awareness of His person.

For Gideon that was crucial. If he was to carry out the
enormous commission given to him from on high, he
needed to be at peace about it. He simply had to be sure
that it was in God's strength that he would go into action
against the enemy. He recognized that it was imperative
his campaign against the Midianites should be governed
by God and not by Gideon.

To confirm that this was the case, he promptly set to

work building an altar to the Lord in that special spot beneath the shade of the twisted old oak. It had become sacred ground to Gideon. Wherever a man meets God in personal encounter, the spot is hallowed forever.

There an altar, laid up in rough, uncut stones gathered from the ground, was erected in sincere devotion. It is at the altar that a man meets his Maker. It is at the altar that a man communes with his Creator. It is at the altar that a man finds peace with God and with himself.

Gideon called his pile of stones *Jehovah—Shalom*, meaning "the Lord—my peace." It would ever stand as a private, personal, profound reminder to him that here he had encountered God and found the purpose for his life. But beyond that, it stood, too, as a public proclamation to his family, friends, and neighbors that he was a man set apart. His new and undivided allegiance was to the Lord God of Israel—not to Baalim, Ashtaroth, or any of the other false gods adored and venerated by his contemporaries.

At that point in his life, he had parted ways with the past. He had changed direction in his drives. He had burned his bridges behind him. He had been converted from a craven coward in the pit of self-pity to a giant under God's great hand.

4

Gideon's Consecration

It was that very same evening of this monumental day in Gideon's life that the word of the Lord came to him regarding his next move. God had found Himself a man who was utterly available to His purposes, obedient to His will. He had found a man daring enough to comply with His commands. In that man and through him He would accomplish astonishing exploits in Israel.

It is ever thus with God.

His eyes run to and fro across all the earth eternally on the lookout for anyone who is open and sensitive to His gracious Spirit. Who will cooperate with His wishes and thus become identified with His purposes on the planet?

Sometimes the intentions of God for His people can be extremely upsetting and deeply disturbing. They are like a mighty earthquake shaking and unsettling all the tired old traditions and deadening habits of our lives and homes. It simply must be so if there is to be a new direction and drive to our endeavors.

The Lord simply does not pour the new wine of His life

into the cracked and leaking old wineskins of our dry little lives. He does not stitch the fresh new cloak of His own character to the tattered, weakened cloth of our old characters. There must be a total renewal that begins at the central core of the inner citadel of our makeup. Eventually it extends to take in the entirety of our beings so that the net result is a total transformation of the person. As it has been put so powerfully by Paul in 2 Corinthians 5:17, 18: "Therefore if any man be in Christ, he is a new creature [creation]: old things are passed away; behold, all things are become new. And all things are of God . . . ."

With Gideon this titanic transformation was to begin with the false gods of his family—Baal and Ashtaroth. They simply had to go. There could no longer be any sort of cozy, accommodating compromise with these pagan effigies. They had to be torn from their place of prominence among His people. God's first command from fire-filled Mount Sinai to His servant Moses had been: *"You will have no other gods before Me!"* And that edict still stood unchanged.

This very night Gideon would tear down the great family altar to Baal erected by his father's household. He would—true to his own name, "the cutter down"—chop down the sacred grove and idol totem pole planted in honor of Ashtaroth. All that stood for subservience to these gods of affluence, sex, violence, and licentiousness would have to be supplanted by an altar to Jehovah, the living and true God of Israel.

This was no simple thing to do: to fly in the face of his family's sacred rites; to risk the rage of his father's fury; to challenge the customs of his entire community with utter impunity was to invite dreadful consequences. It could very well mean incurring not only the displeasure and

angry hostility of his own home and family but also cruel
censure from the whole community. In fact it could very
well cost him his life.

The cost of following the Lord is always high. The challenge to become one of His loyal ones is ever lofty. The
high road of holy, wholesome living to which He calls
men is not strewn with rose petals. It is a tough trail,
rocky and rugged with the stern stones of divine demands. Christ made this very clear when He was among
us. He insisted that God's claim upon His chosen men of
valor supersede any made upon them by their family or
friends. He simply insisted upon prior place in their affection. For to have met and found God was to have encountered the explosive force of a new-found affection in life.

This is precisely what had happened to Gideon under
the dusty, old oak that day. So this very night, with calm
composure and irrepressible intent, he set out to demolish the last vestige of the spurious, counterfeit gods.
The last shred of devotion to any strange deity would be
torn from the citadel of his affections, and that of his family.

Courage—calm, cool, calculating courage—carries with
it an enormous contagion. It is its own best advertise-
ment. And apparently this young countryman had no difficulty at all enlisting the help of ten others to carry out his
daring adventure in the dark. Even though the ten men
were his father's servants, they, too, under Gideon's gallant leadership, readily threw in their lot with the bold
young man. They quickly yoked up their master's bull
with a second one, seven years of age.

These bulls, like the kid Gideon had sacrificed that day,
must have been kept hidden in some secret enclosure or
cave. At least up to this point they had escaped the prying

eyes of the rapacious Midianites. Perhaps, as is often done in very hot countries, they had often been teamed up at night to do the plowing under moonlight when heat and flies were absent. Then the work went much easier both for owner and beast.

In any case Gideon and his ten accomplices led the powerful team down to the giant altar of Baal under cover of darkness. What had to be done had to be done swiftly and surely. An air of intense excitement gripped the gang. They were bent on a dangerous mission. It could mean their lives, but there was no turning back or to the side. The God of Gideon, the God of Israel, the God who brought fire from the rock to consume the sacrifice was among them. His presence was there. His person was real. His power was evident and apparent to His people. What He said, they would do without question or debate.

The straining team was hitched to strong ropes secured around the great stone monolith. At first it refused to budge. But as the drivers shouted to their beasts and lashed them with their whips, mighty muscles swelled and tendons strained until finally the great stone structure began to totter. With a resounding rumble, it tumbled to the earth in a cloud of dust and debris.

Under Gideon's guidance the very last vestiges of the pagan altar were razed to the ground. Not a single chip of stone remained standing upon another.

In its place Gideon carefully instructed his companions to collect twelve large, similar-sized, rough, uncut boulders from his father's rocky fields. These he ordered to be laid up carefully in three tiers of four stones each. This altar stood strong as a symbol of communion between the twelve tribes of Israel and their God. Always this had been the traditional form taken by his people in direct compliance with the command of Jehovah.

The altar was erected with great care upon the large smooth rock upon which earlier in the day he had offered his personal sacrifice to his angelic visitor. That was its foundation. So when the work was done, the structure stood strong and sturdy beneath the stars. It had been a big job—not easy to carry out in the dark while all his friends and family slept soundly beneath their blankets.

Very often the greatest accomplishments for God are carried out in the quietness of our own inner lives. There, away from the view of our contemporaries, we carry out the private and personal commitments entrusted to us by the Lord. While others around us may be sound asleep, we are on the go for God. It is not necessarily a case of indulging in personal daring. It is not a matter of brazen bravado. It is simply a question of doing what the Lord asks us to do.

Gideon then instructed his men to take their axes to the sacred grove and totem tree. It was an eerie sound to hear the sharp metal tools tearing and slicing into the tough wood. It was surprising the chopping did not awaken the village. When the timber crashed to the ground, heavy thuds shook the earth.

It was Gideon's first great hour of glory. The false gods were down, torn from their positions of prominence. A grin of glee spread across his strong features. All had gone well. There remained only one last step, then his assignment was complete. He ordered the felled wood to be chopped into fuel. The seven-year-old bullock that had survived seven years of Midianite occupation would be butchered. A supreme sacrifice of its flesh would be made to Jehovah upon the newly built altar. This sacrifice of a bullock was the sacrifice of sin for a man's entire family and nation.

The action was not lost on his men. They were well aware of its implications. This ritual, carried out under cover of darkness, was an atonement being made on behalf of the perverseness of their people. It was a sin offering for a nation that had rejected and repudiated their God and their Redeemer.

As the flames on the altar licked at the flesh and consumed the fat, its pungent aroma filled the night air. The commingled fragrance of wood smoke and roasting meat drifted into the night sky. It wafted here and there on the night breezes. For seven long, tedious, torturous years no such spectacle had been seen in Israel.

By the light of the flickering fire on the altar, Gideon and his men saw to it that not a scrap of wood from the Asherah remained. Every chip was burned. And not a shred of meat remained. The cleansing fire consumed all. As the day dawned with streaks of crimson light in the east, only a bed of ashes cooled on the newly erected altar.

For Gideon this had been his first giant step following God. It stood for his total consecration to the call of Jehovah. He was no longer just one of the crowd. He was a man set apart for special service. He was a leader now singled out to save his people. He had cleared the decks of his life from any counterfeit complications. He had come clean with God. The idols in his life were torn away. He was a man ready for action, prepared and purified for combat. Nothing remained to drag him down or hobble his movements.

He was free to follow God, very God.

He was free to fight great battles.

He was free to face the enemy unafraid.

He was free from divided affections or diluted loyalties. He was free to triumph.

For Gideon this was the dawning of a new day. He had never been this way before.

Likewise for his kinsmen and fellow villagers, it was the beginning of a new era in their experience. None of us can live as islands to ourselves. Invariably our conduct and characters make an enormous impact for good or evil upon our contemporaries. *And* Gideon's actions, like a pebble dropped into the quiet waters of their stagnant lives, would send waves of repercussion to the very extremity of their little world.

"Who has done this dastardly thing?" The villagers shouted angrily when they saw what had happened in the night. "Who has torn down the altar to Baal, razed the Asherah, and erected a new altar in its place?" Their eyes flamed and their voices were raised in a high, screaming crescendo of vituperation.

"Whoever the iconoclast is, he must die." They yelled vehemently. "No one dare to do this dreadful deed without paying the supreme penalty."

"Gideon must die! Gideon must die!" They shouted in unison. It was a cry to be echoed eight hundred years later outside of Pilate's hall in Jerusalem. It is ever the cry of a people who will neither recognize nor receive the true and living Lord.

The gray-haired Joash, venerated, old gentleman that he was in the community and clan of the Abiezerites, was challenged to deliver his son Gideon. The young man must die. He could not be allowed to upset the status quo of their staid little society.

But Joash, too, had been touched with the transforming dynamic of the new life in his son. To put it into our modern parlance, he had long yearned for a renewal of "the old time religion." His old heart hankered for a word from heaven. He had ached deep inside for a manifestation of the power and presence of Jehovah God. It had seemed so long, too long in truth, since the Lord had laid bare His great arm to save His people from their peril.

What Gideon had done quickened his father's faith. It stirred his slumbering spirit. It startled his sleepy soul.

With enormous audacity and courage he challenged the attackers. "If Baal, your god, be a true god, let him defend himself. If he is authentic, let him protect himself."

It was a startling counterattack. His antagonists were thrown into disarray. It was one thing for young Gideon to undertake great exploits for God. It was quite another for his venerable father to endorse what he did with such virile vehemence.

Godliness polarizes people. As the might and power and presence of God's Spirit became manifest in this man, those around him were immediately divided. Some would be loyal, others not.

Out of enormous respect and admiration, Joash nicknamed his son *Jerubbaal,* meaning, "the one who has beaten Baal."

It was a term of high esteem and deep affection, welding father and son in Gideon's first great escapade for God.

5

Gideon's Call to Arms

IT WAS JUST at this crucial juncture in the personal life of Gideon that a massive movement of enemy forces got • under way. Not only did the Midianites decide to overrun Israel again, but they brought with them allies from among the Amalekites and desert bedouin. A gigantic alliance of hostile forces assembled east of the Jordan.

For some of these desert nomads, warring, raiding, and plundering were and ever have been a way of life. Even to this very day the Arab bedouin remain a roving remnant of fierce fighters. Their main preoccupation is the plundering and pillaging of strangers who stray into their territory or neighboring nations. Hawks of the wild wastes, they stoop to the kill with cruel frenzy.

And now the combined forces of these foes, with their warriors mounted on camels, crossed the fords of the Jordan. Like a huge, moving, sinister swarm of devouring locusts, they swarmed up the valley of Jezreel. This was to penetrate the very heartland of Israel. This rich and fertile valley ran west like a giant corridor to the shining waters of the Mediterranean. It was the great open central invasion route that would enable an invader to cut Israel in half, dividing her forces. It is the same valley in which ultimately the great battle of Armageddon will be fought.

After seven years of occupation and oppression Israel's plight appeared hopeless and precarious. It seemed inevitable that she would be wiped out as a people. Surely this would have been the case but for the active intervention of the Spirit of the living God. Eternally alert, ever active, He was awake to the peril of God's chosen people, and in this hour of crisis came upon Gideon.

To us moderns who are conditioned to success being measured in size, scale, and superiority of numbers, it is difficult to grasp God's ways. His economy is, to put it rather bluntly, very baffling to human beings. He does not depend upon the masses or overwhelming forces to achieve His ends. Rather He looks for a man here or a woman there through whom His purposes are accomplished. It has ever been His way.

Under the impulse of God's own Spirit, Gideon quite literally became a man "clothed" in the person of the Lord. But even more, as one of the very moving, older translations puts it, "The Spirit of the Lord clothed Himself" with Gideon. Put in plain language we would say that Gideon was both surrounded and permeated by the divine presence of God. He was in God, and God was in him. Or as our Lord stated so simply, "I in you, and you in Me."

Here at last God had found a man in whom He could move mightily. He had invaded a life through which His purposes could be realized with resounding success. God does not need or want our human skills, expertise, or resources. He wants us: our wills, our loyalty, our love, our implicit cooperation and obedience.

Under the direction and inspiration of God's guidance, Gideon, the plain, unpretentious countryman, blew a trumpet. It was the ancient battle call to arms. This was something generals and military commanders did, not simple farm folk. Yet its effect was electrifying. Like chain lightening flashing across a black and stormy sky, the war cry coming from Gideon blazed across the country. It galvanized Israel into action.

Such a bugle blast had not been heard for seven long dreary, dusty years. The battle cry had been a note muted and missing. The call to arms was a shout that stirred the blood. Beginning with his own little clan of Abiezer, men dropped their sickles and shears to pick up swords and spears.

Gideon suddenly found himself the central catalyst around which enormous activity was precipitated. Men armed to the teeth gravitated to him from all around. Even those who the day before were determined to take his life for throwing down the altar to Baal, turned about full face now to lend him their allegiance.

It was an unbelievable spectacle. No such drama had stirred Israel for a generation. Foot runners sped away to the far corners of his own tribe Manasseh calling his compatriots into action. Other messengers raced breathlessly into Asher, Zebulun, and Naphtali, summoning men to arms.

Strange as it seems there was an immediate response. Some thirty-two thousand would-be warriors left their fields, their farms, their families, and their flocks to heed the rallying cry of their obscure countryman—a man whom most of them had never even heard of before. In all the war annals of Israel this was perhaps the most remarkable call to arms ever witnessed.

Perhaps from our perspective it is well to pause here briefly and discover what the divine principle is that was at work. For this was no ordinary conscription of men for combat. It was not a methodical, man-made recruitment of military personnel. It was rather the marshaling and mobilization of a nation under supernatural impulse. Thousands upon thousands of hardheaded, downtrodden, discouraged people do not ordinarily volunteer for combat under the inexperienced command of an unknown, untrained novice.

The secret was the source of Gideon's inspiration. Like a swelling stream which alone knows its secret springs in the hills, so Gideon knew his God. It was from God alone that his strength and courage came. Yet that divine life went flooding out to touch and transform uncounted other thousands through this ordinary man. He was but the channel through which God poured His life to inspire and lift an entire nation.

It is when a man's life has its springs in God's Spirit, that there flows from him blessing and inspiration to the ends of the earth. It may well touch, refresh, and revive a host of places or people which up until then knew nothing of its source.

It had been Gideon's intimate, firsthand contact with the living God in personal encounter that supplied the enormous momentum of the moment. Not only had God given him the courage to overturn the inertia of his times but also to inject an aura of adventure into his contemporaries. It was the obvious call of God upon him and the "rightness" of the time that rallied Israel's disorganized, ragtag forces to his side. He had suddenly been catapulted into the role of a popular revolutionary who would smash to pieces then tear away the cruel yoke of their oppressors.

Beyond this Gideon had to have the guidance of God to put in place once more the Lordship of Jehovah. If he was to be a great man of valor, it meant more than merely casting off the tyranny of Midian. It also implied that the Kingship of God had to be reestablished among his people. A revolutionary, to stand tall in history, must provide his nation with something superior to what he destroyed. It is not enough to just tear down and demolish. One must then go on to lay a new foundation. One must erect a new structure superior to its predecessor for the good of all.

As Gideon looked into the faces of the voluntary forces gathering around him, he could see no great assurance of victory. Many of the men were but untaught, untrained youths who perhaps for the first time had picked up a sword or grasped their fathers' spears to do battle. The weapons were awkward and unwieldy in their still soft and unsure grasps.

Many of these fellows were, like himself, farm lads who came to his call eagerly but also very frightened. They had never been baptized in the bloodbath of war. Some looked more like lambs ready for slaughter than lions prepared to pounce upon their prey.

Gideon knew all too well the divided and disunited condition of his country. Already fierce rivalries and deep smoldering jealousy burned between the lesser tribes, like his own, and the more powerful ones of Ephraim and Judah. In fact he had not even dared to call on them for help in this dangerous mission. He would have been scoffed at with derision. They were too proud, too haughty, too superior to submit themselves to an "unknown" leader like himself.

No, if he was to join battle with the enemy, he would pretty well have to go it alone. He could not even rely on the priesthood of his people for spiritual support. The tribe of Levi was conspicuous for its obvious absence in any advances made against the forces of evil. The judges who preceded Gideon had been drawn from among the laity. Like himself, they were the common clay of the common people, out of which God had chosen to shape vessels of special and noble service to society.

Gideon may have been a simple son of the soil, but he was no simpleton. He may have been a humble landsman, but he was no ignorant lout. He may have been a farm fellow with some failings, but he was no fool.

He was an honest, genuine man at the heart of this great movement in Israel. He knew with deep and unshakable conviction that victory would depend not on Gideon but on God. He was acutely aware that if Israel was to survive and flourish, her salvation must come from above. The presence and power of Jehovah had to be with his people if they were to prosper in this tremendous undertaking.

It was for this reason, and only this, that Gideon that night put out his fleece upon the hot, parched ground. He needed proof positive that it would be God Himself who was to save Israel from the enemy hordes now camped in the very heartland of this country. He had to be assured that God's presence would go with him as he led this motley mob of men into battle.

Earlier that day he had cast his eye across the broad, sweeping plain of Jezreel. What he saw there would have made any lesser man's courage turn to water. The black, goatskin tents of the bedouin covered the ground like an ominous dark shadow. The amassed multitudes of the Midianites spread across the landscape like a formidable swarm of vociferous locusts consuming everything in sight. The ominous might of the enemy was enough to strike stark white terror into his own trembling heart.

His help must come from God.

His direction must be divine.

His leadership must come from the Lord.

At sundown Gideon stretched his fleece of wool on the dust outside his home. He laid it, significantly, upon the very spot where he first stood amid the dust and chaff of his threshing floor when the angel of the Lord came to him. He was going back to his own beginnings with God. He was returning to the very point at which Jehovah had promised to be with him.

Gideon identified himself with his fleece. It was his fleece. And in that fleece he saw himself stretched out before his God. He was waiting quietly for the divine dew of God's gracious Spirit to descend and rest upon him. This he expected; this he anticipated; this he must have.

Just as Moses of old had cried out to God, "I will not go hence and lead this nation unless *Thy presence go with me*," so now the same plea came from Gideon. God had declared often to Israel, "I will be as the dew unto Israel!" And Gideon claimed that commitment for himself.

Even though it was harvest time, even though it was hot and arid with summer sun, even though dew seldom lay on the ground these still mornings, Gideon came out at dawn to find his fleece soaking wet. It was more than merely damp. It was saturated.

God's confirmation to the young man was, "Though all around you is a people dry spiritually and desiccated morally, My Spirit has descended, fills, and saturates your soul. Assuredly I am with you. I go with you. I send you. I lead you."

In a gesture of commingled joy and courage, Gideon gathered up the fleece in his big brown fists. He wrung it out with a great twisting action of his sinewy arms. Jubilantly he collected the water in his bowl—the same empty gravy bowl from which he had poured out his broth to the Lord a few days before.

God does not delay in filling what is emptied. He quickly replaces with His own free, flowing life any part of life that is vacated for His presence to possess. Gideon's gravy had been replaced with God's glory.

But that in itself was not enough. The following evening he entreated God to allow him to reverse the ritual. Again the fleece would be spread out on the dusty threshing floor. God be pleased that though it should remain dry, all around would be wet with dew from heaven.

And it was so!

To Gideon this was ample confirmation that even if he himself might later fail or become dry, God's blessing and refreshment would in fact still fall upon and revive all of Israel around him—this though they were dry as dust in their present spiritual state.

Again the proof was provided. The Lord would be with Israel. All the ground was wet the next morning. In the strength of that assurance Gideon went to war. His faith had been confirmed. *His trust was in God.*

6

Gideon Prepares for Battle

ONCE GIDEON HAD RECEIVED positive confirmation from the Lord, by way of the fleece, that the war with Midian was in God's plan, he lost no time preparing for combat. In fact it was the alacrity and promptness with which Gideon obeyed God that accounted for his great victory over the enemy. Once his course of action was clear, he did not delay or drag his heels in carrying out his commission.

It is terribly important to grasp this basic principle. Too often, even when we know what God's wishes are for us, we tend to vacillate in our decisions. We merely entertain the idea of doing that which has been requested of us. We toy with the commands of God. We turn them over and over in our minds viewing them from every angle as though they were playthings given to us purely for pleasure or self-indulgence.

To do this is to play games with God. It is really an enormous affront to Him. It represents colossal conceit on our part. And invariably the net result is that the purposes for our lives in the planned economy of the Lord are thwarted and frustrated. It is only His gracious and marvelous patience with our petty perverseness that saves us from irrevocable disaster.

Gideon had been given the go-ahead sign from God. He did not hold back from preparing for battle. There was a war to be won. There was a fierce contest to be fought. There was an opponent to be overcome. Sitting around and just talking about battle tactics would never do the job. His directives were coming from above. Jehovah God was going with him. He would move into action. His confidence was in the Lord. He would advance in faith no matter how overwhelming the enemy forces.

So at dawn the next day he and his irregular army of thirty-two thousand men made their first great camp at the well of Harod. It was situated across the great valley of Jezreel opposite Moreh where the Midianites were already encamped. It was possible in the clear morning light to look across the fertile plain and see the foe mustered on the far side in their massed hordes. It was a threatening sight, fearsome enough to make Gideon's untrained men tremble in their sandals.

Even the name of the watering place, *Harod*, was in no way reassuring, for it meant "the place of trembling." Already some of the new recruits began to have second thoughts about being there. It was one thing to boast proudly about breaking off the enemy bonds while back home in their caves, dens, and underground dugouts, but it was a totally different thing to stand here on the edge of the open plain imagining what it would be like to engage in hand-to-hand combat with the enemy cavalry mounted on camels. Even the best of Gideon's warriors had been unable to bring along a donkey, let alone such sophisticated war equipment as horses or chariots.

No, indeed, the prospects were far from promising. In fact they were downright frightening. Many of Gideon's men were quite sure they would be slaughtered on this plain by the overwhelmingly superior enemy forces. A mood of despair spread among them. Whispers of foreboding filtered through the ranks of massed men. The contagion of craven fear began to spread from one to another.

The Lord God was not the least perturbed by this. He knew it would happen. Like most of us, these timid men could see only the terrible threat of their circumstances. Their whole attention was focused on the foe—not on the One who would lead them to triumph.

"You have far too many troops!" was the blunt, blood-chilling declaration of Gideon's divine Commander. It was an assessment of the situation that would have shattered the confidence in any lesser man.

"Too many troops?" If it had not been such an appalling appraisal, it might have been laughable. But Gideon knew better by now than to dismiss the Lord lightly, or laugh at His declarations.

"I will not permit Israel to overthrow Midian with such a mass of men. Inevitably it would give them grounds for boasting about their own prowess in war. Send home the shaky-kneed soldiers!"

Gideon, his own heart a little aflutter, could quite easily have tossed in the towel at this point. It was one thing to go into battle with a reasonable array of military might. It was quite another to look like a fool taking on a formidable foe who had overwhelming odds in their favor.

Again Gideon did not debate the issue. He did not draw back in despair. He did not question his commands.

He had been given clear, explicit orders. He would comply and carry them out no matter what the cost.

Without flinching he issued immediate instructions to his men. "Anyone who is the least bit fearful or afraid to face the foe is free to go home!" It is doubtful indeed if ever in the entire history of war, such an incredible order had been given by a commanding officer. This sort of thing just is not done. Always the opposite is true. No man is ever spared who might possibly lend increased might and power to the offensive.

For Gideon the next couple of hours must have been the epitome of agony. First a few of the most fainthearted picked up their weapons of war, and with a low murmur, turned their backs to their companions as they headed for home. Their action spurred others to follow suit and soon a stream of the finest fighting men moved away en masse. In fact twenty-two thousand turned tail to return to their families and farms.

In a single morning Gideon had been stripped of nearly two-thirds of his armed forces. Any other general would have called it quits. All that were left to him was the equivalent of a single division of ten thousand untrained troops.

If most of us had been placed in this man's unenviable position, we would have been very sure that God had had His wires all crossed up. But the Lord's lines of communication were very clear. He knew what He was doing. Gideon did not doubt it. This in itself is a remarkable tribute to the man's unshakable confidence in God. He did not question what was happening. He simply proceeded step by step to do as he was told.

This precisely was the secret to his ultimate success. It is only the person prepared and willing to comply promptly with the immediate wishes of God at the moment who can be sure of clear direction and light for guidance further down the road. So many of us seek for illumination for the days ahead while adamantly refusing to make a move in deference to God's desires in the present moment. We wonder why we seem to be in darkness, our feet mired in the circumstances about us. The answer simply is that God gives no light for the future if we are unprepared to walk in the light He gives us for the present. Five minutes of implicit obedience to God's will can reveal more truth to us than a month of mulling over what it is we think or suppose we should do with our own little affairs.

God did not leave Gideon long in doubt as to what his next move should be. As if the first culling of his forces was not enough, there was to be an even further reduction in numbers. Surely this would be utterly calamitous. How could he possibly hope to succeed if he was to be so fearfully stripped?

God's ways and men's ways are simply not the same. His thoughts and ours are very often diametrically opposite. His view and our views are so utterly divergent as to seem well nigh irreconcilable. His economy and our techniques are totally different. His methods and man's methods are miles apart. In His love and concern for us, God invites us to allow our minds to be transformed into His. He calls us to abandon our fallible human technology for His tactics. Few of us ever really do.

Our little fears of failure, our petty pride of personal success, our self-centered determination to do our own thing turn us again and again to try our own techniques, to rely on our own man-made methodology to accomplish God's work in the world. We fall flat in our endeavors, then wonder what went wrong.

Happily for Gideon this was not the case.

In this hour of crisis for himself, as a commander, and for his people, as a nation, he looked only to the Lord for leadership. His authority came from God. His signals conveyed by God's own gracious, sovereign Spirit were coming in clear and ungarbled. Gideon was a man under command. He was a man on the move for God. He was a man not to be deflected or diverted in any degree from the divine decrees coming to him from above.

It was a crucial hour for Israel.

It was no time for divided opinions.

It was the point at which only divine direction could deliver this people from their despair and ignominy as a downtrodden race.

"But Gideon, the remaining ten thousand troops are still far too great a force!" The declaration might have seemed like sheer madness to most men. The allied forces of the Midianites, Amalekites, and bedouin encamped across the plain numbered well over 135,000. It would have been tough enough to engage them with all his original army of 32,000. Now that he was left with only ten thousand, the odds already against him were about fourteen to one. And still the Lord insisted he had too many.

Gallant general that he was, Gideon was undaunted. He did not for a moment question God's clear directions. He took his troops down to drink as he was directed. There the Lord Himself would select the elite corps of commandos who would carry out this daring assignment. At least Gideon could be sure of one thing: if they were hand-picked by God, they were bound to be the best. Or were they?

Of the twenty-two thousand men who earlier in the day

had returned home, the majority had been the fierce
fighters of Gilead—notorious for their courage in combat.
Now that another large group was to be called from the
ranks, the tiny handful that finally remained at best might
seem like a contemptible remnant.

Again it was a question of God's choice of people for
accomplishing His ends being quite different from ours.
So often those whom He selects to achieve great things are
the last we would ever think to choose. God does not look
on our outward appearance. He sees far beyond our obvious accomplishments or attainments. He seeks for those
of honest spirit and open availability to do His work in
the world.

This principle is stated clearly by Paul in writing to the
church at Corinth:

> For ye see your calling, brethren,
> how that not many wise men after the flesh,
> not many mighty, not many noble, are called:
> But God hath chosen the foolish things
> of the world to confound the wise;
> and God hath chosen the weak things
> of the world to confound the things
> which are mighty;
> And base things of the world, and things
> which are despised, hath God chosen,
> yea, and things which are not,
> to bring to nought things that are.
>   1 Corinthians 1:26–28

And it was the same concept at work in God's own
selection of three hundred special men for the initial raid
on the enemy camp that night.

When the men followed Gideon down to drink from the water troughs beside the well of Harod, they were watched very carefully.

Out of ten thousand, only three hundred would lap up the water like a thirsty dog running through a stream, picking up refreshment, while hot on the trail of the prey. It was no special honor to be so singled out. Even to be likened to a dog in any way was to be very much maligned. In Israelite culture a dog was a creature of contempt. To be identified even very indirectly with a dog was to be scorned and humiliated. It was in short to be considered contemptible.

Yet, these were the men chosen that hot afternoon, by divine edict, to perform great exploits for God. It is really remarkable that Gideon still did not debate the issue. His unshakable faith in the Eternal One stirs our deepest admiration.

It could, of course, be argued that Gideon was better off to be rid of the 9,700 men who stooped down to drink deeply from the refreshing water. It has been pointed out that the troops on the verge of battle who allowed themselves to become completely absorbed in slaking their thirst really were not battle ready. They were not fully on guard. Their attention from the enemy had been diverted by self-indulgence in refreshment.

This may all be true to a degree. Still the point remains that the great test here really was not so much with the men themselves, as it was of Gideon's faith in God. For when this sorting of his forces was finished, this rough-hewn, uncomplicated countryman had only three hundred armed men still standing with him. The combat ratio had now been reduced to the ridiculous figure of 1:450. Put another way, for every fighting man who would go into action with him that night, the enemy was fielding 450 fierce warriors.

Never, ever, in the annals of warfare had the odds been so totally overwhelming. Though it is significant that in the great contest on Mount Carmel, between Elijah and the false prophets of Baal and Ashtaroth, the odds were equally formidable. For there alone, Elijah challenged and overwhelmed 450 false prophets under the direct command of God. The ratio was identical.

It is also of significance that out of the original forces mustered to his side, Gideon now had somewhat less than 1 percent of his men remaining. As God had done before, and as He always does, He was to show that one man with God is a majority. He was to prove that little, very little, can be much, so very much, when God is in it.

It takes faith really to believe this.

It calls for implicit confidence to act on it.

Yet, this is the response God ever looks for from His people. Because always, ever, it is the honor and glory of His character to vindicate and validate the faith of any person who invests his trust in Him. He cannot do otherwise than honor both Himself and those who obey Him.

This Gideon knew!

7

The Bit of Barley Bread

Events had moved rapidly for Gideon that day. It had been a bit devastating to be stripped of almost all his military forces. No doubt as the evening shadows lengthened across the dusty plain of Jezreel, he wondered rather fearfully just what this awesome night might hold. The sun, setting like a distant flaming fire over the western sea, was a red reminder that tomorrow might just be a better day.

But Gideon's hope really did not rest in any natural phenomena. His confidence, if he had any at this point, did not reside in the three hundred men of valor left with him. His faith for the future lay, not in what could be seen, but in the unshakable commitment of God to him.

Repeatedly the Lord had reassured Gideon that He would go with him against the enemy. He had assured this young farmer that it was He who would save Israel by His great outstretched arm. And now once again He was to confirm this for the youthful leader who may have felt a bit forsaken and forlorn. He was instructed to make a private sortie into the enemy camp after dark. It would be a most daring and dangerous maneuver.

Perhaps Gideon's courageous heart missed a beat or two at the thought of creeping stealthily through the enemy lines. He was not at all happy with the idea of worming his way through the guards on watch. One misstep, one false move in the dark, and a Midianite spear would be plunged between his ribs. Besides, there was the horde of camels. He would have to creep past their great hulking forms in the gloom. Only one or two would have to groan uneasily or shuffle to their feet in fright and his game would be up. No, this command called for more cold-blooded courage than open hand-to-hand combat ever did.

God, who had Gideon's own best interest in mind, was fully aware of the chill, clammy fear that fastened its fist around his frightened heart. He knew that this was a terribly tough assignment. But He also knew that Gideon would not back away from it, especially if he could take his servant Purah along as a companion on this hazardous mission.

It is ever reassuring for God's people to remind themselves that the Lord knows us better than we know ourselves. He is completely acquainted with the strengths and weaknesses of our unpredictable characters. He never exposes us to tests or puts us into situations beyond our ability to handle. He deals with us in infinite integrity. And because He is God, whatever He demands of us is ultimately for the maximum benefit of both ourselves and those around us.

In this particular adventure Purah was the loyal servant selected to accompany Gideon. He had, like the three hundred other fighting men, been literally singled out by

God for this risky assignment. His name Purah meant
"fruitful" or "the productive person." He was to be Gideon's right-hand man for moral support and encouragement. His greatest gift to Gideon that night was simply
being there as a helpful witness to what went on. As with
many of God's choicest, unsung souls, this simple servant's great gift from the Lord was just that of being a
help, an encouragement, when the going got very tough.
His moral support was something especially precious
amid the perils of the night.

Together the two men started off across the valley of
Jezreel. As they stole across the wide plain toward Moreh,
they both recalled God's great promise to Abraham on
that very spot almost exactly one thousand years before. It
was at Moreh, when Abraham's gaze fell first across this
fertile land, that God had appeared to him and declared
positively: "I will give this land unto thy seed." In humble gratitude Abraham built his first altar there and gave
thanks for this assurance.

Deep within their hearts, the two Israelites believed
that God would again make good on that ancient promise
to His people. Even though they could see the flickering
flames of the enemy campfires, and hear the low rumble
of movement in the enemy lines, hope leaped in their
spirits. God, their Lord Jehovah, who had been faithful to
Abraham, Isaac, Jacob, Joseph, Moses, Joshua, and all the
judges would be true to them this dangerous night.

Gideon and Purah could not be content merely to reconnoiter the enemy position in a casual sort of way. They
had been sent there actually to penetrate the lines and
discover what the mood of the Midianites might be. It
demanded cool courage to crawl on their stomachs past
the outer guards. Stealthily they slithered through the

grass past the camels chewing their cuds with great explosive grunts. Finally, despite the flickering firelight that cast shifting shadows all around them, they lay quietly behind one of the black bedouin tents.

Inside they could hear the animated conversation of its two occupants. Apparently one fellow had fallen asleep earlier in the evening and had a dreadful nightmare. The bad dream had been so disturbing, it woke him up startled and shaken.

"I dreamed this terrible thing," he yawned, rubbing the sleep from his eyes and shaking his head to fully rouse himself. "Of all things a cake of barley bread, a *chapati*, came tumbling into the camp." His eyes widened and his face tensed. "The chapati struck a tent and completely overturned it. In fact despite its guy ropes and poles, it was flattened and lay in a heap on the ground."

It was the impossible sort of thing from which so many dreams are fashioned. Yet, in dismay the soldier shook his head in wonderment and fear. "I just don't understand it."

His companion in the tent must have been a bit of a necromancer. Immediately he had an explanation for the nightmare. This was not uncommon, for the desert tribes dabbled much in signs and portents. They studied the signs of the zodiac under their desert skies, indulging much in fortune-telling and stargazing.

"Your dream means only one thing," the second man spoke with startling assurance. "This overturn of a tent by a tiny bit of barley bread is nothing else than a sign of Gideon's sword." He pulled at his big black beard with nervous fingers. "Gideon is the son of Joash, a man of Israel. Into his strong hand God has already delivered all the hosts of Midian and her allies." The two men in the tent looked at each other uneasily. Panic began to show in their faces. They felt and knew instinctively that as an army, they were beaten even before the battle began.

Outside in the darkness Gideon and Purah nudged each other gleefully. Both of them grinned so widely their strong white teeth shone pale in the shadowy night. What an incredible bit of good cheer this was! It was the sort of thing to lift a man's spirits to singing, his blood to racing, and his body to bursting for battle.

One man with God was a majority!

Two men with God would bear back great good news.

Three hundred men with God would vanquish the enemy.

Faith, hope, and optimism are based, not on that which is observable. They do not depend on the data of physical or material assets. They are grounded in God.

As Gideon and Purah cast their eyes around them, all they could see were thousands of camels. The black hulks of the great ungainly beasts loomed up in the flickering light of the enemy campfires like ten or twenty thousand anthills surrounding them on every side. What a formidable force of cavalry mounts surrounded them on every side.

Beyond that stood the endless ranks of threatening, black bedouin tents. In every one there were fierce and ruthless men of war—warriors armed to the teeth with curved swords, long lances, and deadly daggers. It all might have been terribly terrifying, but God had given Gideon reassurance and confidence.

What if the dream did liken him to a mere bit of barley bread? What did it matter if he was considered of no more consequence than a poor man's chapati? Only livestock, beggars, and lepers partook of barley flour. Any self respecting soul would feed his family on the fine flour milled from the finest wheat. But barley bread—who but the lowest would dine on such crude, humble fare?

Gideon did not mind the gibe. He took no personal offense at the parallel. He was not so proud or haughty as to be hurt by this slur. It is a mark of the man that he concurred with the definition of the dream. He saw himself as really quite insignificant in God's economy. Yet it was in truth his willingness to be nothing that enabled him to become great in God's strong hands.

A man's usefulness to God is directly proportional to his willingness to be counted of little consequence in his own ability or estimation. It is the person who holds no great or grandiose notion of his own worth whom God chooses to achieve great exploits. The very basic reason for this is simply that his own self-importance does not interfere with the ongoing plans of God. The Lord has liberty and joyous freedom to use this individual how and where he chooses with enormous effectiveness.

At this stage in Gideon's meteorlike career, he was malleable material in the Master's mighty hand. He was not blinded or distracted by any self-sufficient conceit. He was not interested in protecting either his own pompousness or prestige. He was simply a sharp and powerful sword in God's great hand.

Because of his implicit, unquestioning, and prompt obedience to the Lord's command, Gideon was now a man fortified with enormous faith. There remained not a shred of doubt in his mind that absolute and ultimate victory over Midian was assured. It simply could not be otherwise. God had given him the omen. He was bound to overcome.

It is worthy of note that the opportunity given to Gideon to move so swiftly from fear to faith was because of his willingness to do precisely what he had been told to do. The Spirit of the living God is given, always in generous measure, to those who comply with God's commands. He shares Himself lavishly with those who cooperate with Him. It is to such that He gives the faith, courage, strength, and serenity of His own presence to perform whatever is asked of them.

There in the shadow of the enemy's black goatskin tent Gideon bowed himself humbly to the ground. In the darkness, with only Purah as a witness, he gave grateful thanks to his God for such a gracious gesture. In reverence and respect he worshiped God the Deliverer of himself and his people.

The reassuring aspect of this entire episode had been the knowledge that God, very God, had been very active and at work behind the scenes. Behind the enemy lines in some remarkable manner, word has swept along the human grapevine that God had singled out Gideon for great exploits. Although previously he may have been an obscure farmer on his marginal land, now suddenly he was assuming the role of a notorious and mighty man of war in Israel.

The stories of Gideon's face-to-face encounter with the Lord had swept across the countryside. Men and women had heard about celestial fire flaming from the rock to consume his sacrifice of meat, bread, and gravy. Tales had been told how Gideon had torn down the venerated altar of Baal and statue to Ashtaroth. The tribes had heard how men in multitudes were willing to take up arms to follow this young revolutionary. Even the incredible account of the fleece had run along the far-flung lines by word-of-mouth messengers. Suddenly *Gideon* had become a household name throughout the camps, without the benefit of mass media.

All of it was part and parcel of the power and influence
of God's Spirit at work behind the scenes. Unknown to
Gideon, the news had even swept across the Jordan into
the enemy encampments of the desert wastes. In the scattered villages and nomadic tent camps, Gideon's prowess
had become a thrilling saga fraught with fearsome consequences for his foes.

Partly, this was why the Midianites had swept back
into Palestine with their Amalekite and bedouin allies at
the time. They hoped to suppress and crush any popular
uprising that might erupt in Israel. They were sure they
could again grind Israel into the ground. But God had
other designs. He had heard the pleas of His people. He
had found a great man in Gideon. So now the tables were
to be turned and all the world would wonder at His work.

For all of us who are God's children it is tremendously
helpful to realize that the Lord, by His Spirit, never slum-
bers nor sleeps. He is not indolent or idle. He does not
neglect those who trust in Him. He is, instead, tremendously active and at work on their behalf. Often we are
totally unaware of where or how our God may be arrang-
ing matters on our behalf. But He does. Frequently the net
result astonishes us beyond our fondest hopes or wildest
dreams.

That night Gideon and Purah slipped away safely
through the enemy lines. They sped back swiftly across
the plain to the Israelite camp at Moreh. In breathless
excitement and with blazing eyes Gideon shouted to his
sleepy stalwarts: "Arise—the Lord has delivered the hosts
of Midian into your hand!"

It was a ringing note of triumph. It galvanized his three
hundred warriors into terrible tigers eager now to pounce
on their prey.

8

Attack at Midnight

GIDEON'S RESONANT BATTLE CRY, "The Lord has delivered the hosts of Midian into your hand," was picked up by his men. It became their war cry, their battle song. This was to be a conquest in which they all shared. It was no one-man show. It was the Lord who was their commander in chief. It was He who would see them all become jubilant victors.

The events of the next few hours of this dramatic night moved with dazzling speed. Gideon was now an inspired general. Using his native wit and keen intellect, under the guidance of God's own Spirit, who indwelt him so abundantly, he acted with enormous commanding authority. Quickly he ordered his three hundred picked men into three companies of a hundred each.

Gathering up earthenware containers from among the whole host that had gathered at Harod, he issued an empty clay pitcher to each combatant. The men had brought provisions in these vessels now being turned over to another use. Similarly he ordered each man to be equipped with a torch that was carried inside the clay container. These were to be borne in their left hands.

In each man's right hand there was placed a crude

71

trumpet. Most of these were made from curling ram's horns. They were not the gleaming gold or silver instruments found in temple processions. Rather they were the rough, hand-carved battle bugles carried by common people into combat. The Midianites had long ago stripped Israel of her silver and gold. It had long since been melted down and beaten into beautiful earrings and gorgeous camel chains that were the pride of the desert raiders. These fine and glittering ornaments dangled from the ears of the wild warriors. They tinkled around the necks of their camels, sparkling in the sun and showing off their wealth.

Besides the earthenware pitchers, the smoldering torches concealed inside, and the mountain horns in their right hands, each of Gideon's three hundred stalwarts bore a sharp sword strapped to his side by a broad belt. There would be blood, sweat, and appalling carnage before this action was over.

Gideon was a leader of impressive might this night. Without fanfare or apology, he spoke directly and firmly to his followers. "Look to me for your orders. Whatever I do, you do. When we surround the enemy encampment, coming at it from three different sides, synchronize your actions with those of my company. We will all blow on our trumpets at once. Then shout at the top of your lungs, 'The sword of the Lord and Gideon!' "

Gideon knew the primitive superstitions of the desert tribes well enough to realize this sort of surprise attack would utterly demoralize them. Those who dabbled in the occult and regulated their lives by signs and portents could easily be panicked in the dark. His sortie with Purah had already disclosed to him that a mood of fear and foreboding was doing its deadly work among the foe.

Without further delay Gideon led his little band down into the valley of Jezreel. Stealthily, and as swiftly as the darkness would permit, they crossed the broad plain. In sinister silence they encircled the Midianite camp. The three hundred men formed a very thin, sparse line around the huge conglomerate of black tents, camels, and battle gear.

It was exactly midnight. A new watch of guards had just come on duty. The sleepy-eyed sentinels who had let Gideon and Purah slip through their guard now turned into their tents. But their slumber was to be short-lived. In a few moments the still night air was shattered and split by the resounding blast of 301 wild war horns.

In blind, bewildered panic the desert fighters bolted wide awake. They burst out of their black tents to hear the terrible trumpet blasts barking at them from every side. In heart-chilling consternation they were sure a fierce feud had erupted amid their own ranks. The desert tribesmen never did trust one another. Treachery and intertribal warfare were their way of life. With the flash of a sword, swift as the wink of an eye, one warrior turned upon another to draw blood. It is ever thus where hot passions rule.

In the confusion there arose a sound even more terrifying than the bugle cries. It was the unleashed battle call of Gideon and his men. Lungs bursting, throat muscles swelling, blood surging through their veins, they shouted fiercely, madly, ferociously, "The sword of the Lord and Gideon." The rising, quivering, terrorizing cry was torn from the throats of three hundred unleashed tigers. Their hour of utter triumph had come.

The terrified enemy troops in crazed fear rushed upon each other. Midianite slayed Midianite, Amalekite, or be-

douin in the darkness. Comrade cut down comrade with
no thought of whom he wounded. Shrieks of pain, groans
of agony, and shouts of fear engulfed the whole camp in
chaos. The grumbling camels lurched to their feet and
rushed off riderless. They trod men under their hard
horny hooves, trampled on the fallen, sometimes collided
into tents.

Suddenly an even more astonishing sound shattered
the night. It was the crash and clatter of three hundred
clay pitchers smashing against one another. Gideon's
warriors smashed jar against jar with fragments falling at
their feet. It was a strange, unusual, clanking sound like a
host of manacled ghosts surging around the camp. The
bedouin were utterly petrified with fear. But the worst
was yet to come. Fed by the fresh night air the smoldering
torches burst into flame. The flickering, dancing light
looked like the flames of hell let loose.

It was more than the Midianites could possibly handle.
Never had these desert hawks been so terrorized. In the
flickering, weird, awful light of the flaming flares, they
rushed at each other in unbridled disarray. A mad mania
of fear drove them to desperate ends. The Spirit of God
swept through their ranks producing passionate terror in
a hundred thousand hearts. Men rushed hither and
thither, yelling, screaming, swinging their swords wildly,
felling their friends in a gory bloodbath. It was utter
mayhem.

Around the perimeter of the camp, Gideon's men stood
strong. Each man was in position. They did not panic or
withdraw. Exultingly they blew their trumpets, waved
their torches high, and between bugle blasts, shouted
aloud. Only the great crash of Jericho's walls beneath the
bugle blasts of Israel could ever compare with the cata-

clysmic conquest of this terrible night. Israel had neither heard nor seen such a spectacle for roughly two hundred years.

In those few short hours after midnight the whole of history had been turned around. The oppressor had become the oppressed. The raider had become the savaged. The spoiler had been spoiled. It was a tremendous triumph for the valiant three hundred. But it had been an even greater victory for the Lord God of Israel and His giant, Gideon.

In total disarray the fragmented enemy forces fled off into the dark. Most of the Midianites, their camels having stampeded away, fled on foot. They were heading back home, making for the river fords along the Jordan. In stark panic they retreated eastward towards Bethshittah, "the house of the scourge" (scourged with acacia thorns); Zererath, "the place of oppression"; Abelmeholah, "mourning instead of dancing"; and Tabbath, "the place that was good but is no longer."

For Midian it was a total rout. For Gideon it was total victory.

The conquest of that night has come down to us across the centuries as an outstanding historical event. Yet it is much, much more than just that. It is more than a great tactical victory against overwhelming odds. It is more than the demonstration of superb leadership and unusual intelligence. There were at work in this engagement divine, God-given spiritual principles which we can apply to our lives with enormous benefit.

To begin with, we see that once Gideon was assured of victory, he wasted no time at all moving into action against Midian. It is remarkable that in the span of a single day and night he had sorted out all the forces under his command; he had personally risked great danger to reconnoiter the enemy camp; he had settled on the exact tactics to overthrow the enemy. In short he did not sit around discussing or debating what he should do. He just did it.

There is a tremendous truth here. In our engagements for God there is sometimes far too much talk. It is common for God's people often to get caught up in tiresome deliberations, wearisome meetings, endless committees, and the fatigue of going round and round the bush.

Gideon was essentially a man of action. He heard the voice of the Lord. He knew what was expected of him. He did it. And the results were dramatic.

It is also of great significance that he did not resort to extraspecial techniques or tools to accomplish his assignment. Such commonplace things as earthenware containers, homemade torches, and rams' horns taken from the hill flocks could be collected from family farms and homesteads. He used what was right at hand. He did not go off in search of sophisticated paraphernalia to accomplish his purposes. It was the common shepherd's rod in Moses' hand that broke Egypt's power over Israel. It was the sling and small smooth stone in David's hand that slew Goliath and routed the Philistines. It was the small sardines and little buns in a boy's hands that fed the famished thousands. What God asks of us is not some superspecial or unusual equipment to achieve His ends. He simply asks: "What have you got in your hand? Put it at My disposal. Let Me use it through you to bless a thousand lives."

Too often we tend to forget, overlook, or deliberately ignore the everyday, commonplace things available to us for God's service. In our search for something special or unusual, we lose sight of the fact that our living Lord can take any cup, pen, or tool held in a ready hand and use it to do great things if we will let Him. Our Christ is not in any way confined or constricted except by our human reluctance to let Him have His wondrous way in our cramped little lives.

Another rather remarkable principle we see in this episode is the part played both by the leader and by his followers. Once Gideon was in command he recognized that there rested on him the responsibility for the conduct of his entire corps. It was not a question of, "Don't do as I do; just do as I say," which is all too common among God's people. Rather it was a positive directive that his followers should all, "Do exactly as I do."

Gideon was no armchair tactician. He did not command from a remote headquarters. He identified himself intimately with his men. He was a frontline general. He was in the forefront of the action. He put his own reputation on the line. He risked his very own life.

Our Lord, the Christ, when He was among us, did precisely the same. He said to His followers, "As the Father hath sent me into the world, so send I you." Elsewhere He said, "Lo I am with you always, even to the end of the world."

If any man or woman assumes leadership among God's people, to be truly effective he cannot hold himself aloof from the common crowd in their struggles with sin, Satan, and their own selves. Preachers and teachers must not take refuge in their ivory towers of prestige and privilege; but rather they must get down into the trenches with their troops and tramp the tough trails in their war-torn sandals.

As for Gideon's men, their behavior in this battle stirs

our spirits to the depths. To quote Tennyson: "Ours is not to question 'why.' Ours is but to do or die!"

It had not been the special privilege of these three hundred men to see and know God as Gideon had done. He alone had seen fire come from a rock to consume his sacrifice. He alone had heard the voice of the Lord command him to tear down the altar to Baal and cut down the idol of Ashtaroth. He alone had seen the fleece first drenched with dew, then later left bone dry. He alone, except for Purah, had heard the dream of the barley bread explained. To all of the other three hundred, these revelations had to be accepted and believed on naked faith.

It stands as a remarkable monument to their fortitude that without question or hesitation they went to war in this calm, strong faith. Much more than that, they stood their ground, each man precisely in his place, exactly as commanded. Each had his part to play, and he played it to the hilt. The total result was a stirring triumph.

Not all of us are chosen of God for leadership roles. Not all of us are to be "Gideons." But among us, the laity, it is expected that we will each do our part and be in our place. The whole battle cannot be carried by our leaders. The preacher, teacher, and anyone in command needs the wholehearted cooperation of the common people.

Our responsibility, too, is to blow the bugle—proclaim the Gospel; hold high the torch—live the life of light in a dark world; and shout aloud for the honor of our God. When we do, God will grant victory.

9

Gideon's Diplomacy

Oᴜᴛ ᴏꜰ ᴛʜᴇ ᴄᴏɴꜰᴜꜱɪᴏɴ and carnage of the enemy camp this historic night, God, the Lord Jehovah of Israel, was bringing a tremendous triumph. It was every bit as great a victory for His people as had been the overthrow of the Egyptians at the Red Sea or the downfall of Jericho under Joshua's army. Again the Lord was demonstrating His amazing ability to deliver His own from the oppressor.

The rout of the Midianites at Moreh was much more than just a tactical, military triumph for Gideon's famous "three hundred." It was also an enormous spiritual renewal for all of this downtrodden, woebegone, broken nation of Israel. Even the most obtuse Israelite would realize at once that here the great arm of his God had been made manifest. Here he saw clearly that the hand of the Lord had intervened on behalf of His chosen ones.

It was this fact, perhaps more than any other, which swept through the towns, villages, farms, and strongholds of Manasseh, Naphtali, and Asher. Like a raging brushfire, the news of the night fanned across the country. Armed men tumbled out of their humble homes and hamlets to join the hue and cry after the fleeing enemy forces. Hounds hot on the trail, they pursued their oppressors, cutting them down as they fled eastward toward the Jordan.

The Israelite warriors were no longer the timid men whom Gideon had sent home the day before. They were not the reluctant, unsure soldiers who had chosen to turn tail rather than attack the invaders. The events of this momentous night had injected them with an overwhelming sense of superiority against enormous odds. Even though thousands of the Midianites, Amalekites, and bedouin had butchered each other in the bedlam of their confusion, uncounted other thousands had fled for the Jordan fords.

Whenever they passed an Israelite farm or village in their flight, the residents would pour out to pursue them mercilessly. Terror stricken, the Midianites were shot through with arrows, pierced with spears, and slashed with swords. Shouts of triumph went up on every side, echoing across the valleys and hills, ringing from the rocks, rousing all of Israel.

In that one terrible day some 120 thousand enemy troops were slaughtered. It was an appalling loss of life of gigantic proportions. Even during some of the greatest engagements in World War II, there were not this many casualties in any single day. Despite the ferocious bombings by military aircraft; the use of high-powered artillery and tanks; the enormous firepower of machine guns, mortars, and bazookas, fewer men ever fell in combat in any one twenty-four-hour battle than were cut down under Gideon's savage attack.

Perhaps in all of this the most miraculous part was the

manner in which men of war, who so shortly before had been so abruptly rejected by this novice commander, would again rally to his call. Obviously this was no ordinary human response. Normally their reply would have been to turn from him in disdain with the cutting comment: "If you're such a great general, go ahead and fight your own war!"

Instead a spirit of wholehearted, vigorous cooperation gripped Gideon's countrymen. This, too, was part of the divine work of God's Spirit. It was He who gave the entire people a single mind to win. Momentarily at least their family feuds, clannish quarrels, and intertribal rivalries were forgotten in the brutal battle. Their petty differences were submerged in the exciting chase across the country.

Gideon had presented his people with an enormous and staggering challenge under God. And to their credit, it must be said, they rose to meet the challenge magnificently. There was before them the opportunity for greatness, and they grabbed it.

In all of this Gideon demonstrated unusual insight. He did not rely on just his own tiny handful of men to do the job. He was not so self-centered or proud that he tried to hug this great achievement to himself. He was a big man, a giant of a man, generous enough and gracious enough to call others to share in the spoils and conquest.

He even sent runners into the hill country of Ephraim. That bold, powerful arrogant tribe of the mountain country had always held the other tribes in contempt. Had Gideon invited them to come under his command from the outset, they would have spat in the dust with contempt and laughed in his face. "Follow a farmer from Manasseh! What a joke! Who is Gideon anyway? Where does he come from? Ophrah is nothing—a dusty, dried-up, windblown bit of barren wasteland."

Thousands of years later, when One greater than Gideon was to appear on Israel's center stage of action, there would be similar insults. "Nazareth! That crude, contemptible community in Galilee. Could any good thing come out of Nazareth?"

But Gideon, like our Lord, was not to be dismayed. And when his request for help in the pursuit of the enemy reached Ephraim, they, too, responded with alacrity. As one man, they turned out in full force. Racing full speed, down out of their mountain country, they carried out a swift encircling movement on the Midianites. In military terminology it was a pincer action. It cut off the enemy's escape route by way of the southern fords across the Jordan. The result was the annihilation of hordes of the desert warriors.

It had been a brilliant tactical maneuver. It was executed with expertise and dispatch. All of Ephraim's famous fighters had flung themselves into the fray fearlessly. The upshot was that two of the topflight princes of Midian were captured and slain: Oreb, "the Raven," and Zeeb, "the Wolf."

These were the sort of names common to the desert tribes. They resembled the titles taken so often by our North American Indians and other tribes who live by the hunt. Oreb, "the Raven," had fled for refuge to a great high outcrop of rock where he was killed. Ever after the spot was called "The Rock of the Raven." Zeeb, "the Wolf," on the other hand had gone underground. Like his now-famous opponent, Gideon, who had first found refuge in a winepress, Zeeb also tried to do the same and was slaughtered in the pit. So from then on that place bore the name of "The Winepress of the Wolf."

As was customary in battle, both of the warrior princes were beheaded. Their plumed and ornamented heads, bejeweled with golden earrings dangling, were borne in bloody pride to Gideon. No greater proof could be provided of Ephraim's prowess in war. Ephraim was not a tribe to take a backseat to anyone in battle. She would show the world who could most fiercely swing a sword. She would let Gideon know this was not just his show.

Though it was a day of titanic events and glorious triumph for Israel, it was also an hour of critical uncertainty. It has been well said that not many men can stand success. Too often it goes to their head. The aura of glory and acclaim undoes them. Their little egos are inflated like a thin-walled bubble shining in the sun, about to burst with its own growing grandeur.

Had Gideon been less of a real general, certainly at this point his career might readily have collapsed. For, despite the overwhelming victory granted him by God, the old ugly rivalry with Ephraim raised its grim head again. The venom running dark in the veins of human nature must ever be an absolute abhorrence to God.

It was not enough that He had given Israel such success. It was not enough that the cruel iron yoke of Midian should have been broken from their necks. It was not enough that Jehovah should have given Israel her freedom once again. They still had to grumble and find fault with Gideon.

"Why didn't you include us in your initial battle plans against the enemy? Why didn't you invite us to share in the action?" Their eyes flashed angrily.

Somehow this proud and haughty tribe could never be satisfied. No matter what a man did, it would be wrong. Had Gideon called them, they would have felt insulted.

And now because he hadn't, they were miffed. It was a devastating commentary on human behavior. And it would take the integrity and wisdom of God to pacify such proud and petulant people.

But the Spirit of God had permeated all of Gideon's personality. He had the mind of the Lord. He did not allow his emotions to control his conduct in this crucial crisis. Just one wrong gesture, one wrong move, one wrong word, and he could well precipitate a bloody civil conflict between his own men of Manasseh and Ephraim's hot-headed warriors.

Looking at the blood-blackened heads of Oreb and Zeeb, Gideon spoke with incredible tact. His words fell upon the hot, flaming emotions of his hearers like a summer shower falling upon heated soil and hot rocks.

"What have I done to compare with your classic conquest and capture of the notorious Raven and Wolf? There are their heads in your hands!" All eyes turned to focus on the warrior skulls, surrounded by hovering swarms of flies drawn by the black blood. "God has granted you a glorious victory! Greater is your triumph than mine! It may seem to you not much more than a final gleaning of the grapes, but even then, it far surpasses the finest wine that a country fellow from dusty Abiezer could ever provide!"

It was a masterpiece of diplomacy. At a stroke it disarmed the arrogant men of Ephraim. Their arguments were gone, blown away in the wind of Gideon's goodwill. In gentle, good-natured, humorous humility, he had diffused an explosive confrontation. He had proved himself a peacemaker. He was indeed a son of God (*see* Matthew 5:9).

In this action Gideon had demonstrated his reliance

upon the Lord to resolve a very complex conflict. He had found wisdom far beyond his own to pacify his "brothers." It was an achievement in the moral realm equal to his remarkable accomplishments in the military field. God had indeed found a giant among men. But his greatness lay not in his own native genius but rather in his simple trust in Jehovah.

Appeased and placated, the men of Ephraim dropped the dispute. They had done their bit in the battle and done it well. Gideon recognized and appreciated their part in the fray. They were satisfied, and so was he. All was well between them. There would be peace now for years to come, in fact for forty. If a Nobel Peace Prize had been awarded in 1256 B.C., Gideon would have been the obvious nominee for the honor.

But Gideon was not content to rest on his laurels. A remnant of the Midianites had managed to make good their escape across the Jordan River. About fifteen thousand ragtag ruffians had either waded or swam across the muddy stream, now low because of late-summer drought. Gideon was not content to let them slip away from his sword. They were led by two courageous desert chiefs Zebah and Zalmunna. Cunning and crafty as two hunted hawks, the cruel, haughty warriors were determined to elude Gideon in their desert wastes.

Gideon was not about to give in. He and his gallant three hundred crossed the Jordan. Its cool waters refreshed their hot, tired bodies and aching limbs. They had all been on the go steadily since before midnight the day before. Passing through the murky water, the men lapped it up hurriedly like hounds hot in the hunt, pursuing their prey. They were unrelenting. There was no slowing down. The Midianites would be brought to bay.

Yet, as they pushed on into the sun-blasted hills across the Jordan, their stomachs were pinched with hunger pangs. All day they had been without food of any sort to fortify their famished bodies. They were growing weak and faint with gnawing hunger.

Suddenly they stumbled into a little settlement called Succoth. Here surely they would find supplies to refresh them. Surely the people of Succoth would share some bread and meat with Gideon's half-starved troops. After all they were distantly related and one did not turn away from those in need in time of war—especially so when men had shown such heroism in battle, such determination against impossible odds.

The residents of Succoth were really not impressed by Gideon. Despite his great victory over Midian already; despite his unrelenting pursuit of the Midianite remnant; despite his enormous perseverance in the face of over-whelming obstacles; despite all of his entreaties; they took a neutral stand.

"After all you haven't yet captured Zebah and Zal-munna!" They taunted him sarcastically. "We will simply play it safe. We'll wait and see what really happens."

It may seem to us an absurd position for this little non-descript community to have taken. The people of Succoth were a splinter offshoot from Ephraim. They had deserted their own mountain tribesmen and crossed into the desert wastes beyond the Jordan. There they subsisted at a low level, barely eking out a precarious existence at the mercy of the Midianites who despised them. They were known as those of "No Name" and it might well be added of "No Loyalty."

Like so many people in the world, they were fence sit-ters. They would not be loyal to anyone. They sought the best of both worlds but fell between the two. The strength, stamina, and spiritual drive of Gideon was not for them. They would not align themselves with the enemy either. By their own choosing they had become "speckled birds." As with all such catastrophic choices in life, in the end it would spell their utter undoing.

As a man sows, so shall he reap. Their final end would be a shameful calamity.

10

Gideon's Perseverance

THE NEGATIVE REACTION from Succoth to Gideon's request for refreshments would have daunted some lesser men. But not Gideon, even though at this point he and his men were battle weary, famished, and fatigued. He was a commander strong in the Lord. His confidence lay not in the unpredictable nature of men but in the remarkable reliability of God to sustain and empower him.

Repeatedly his requests for reinforcements from his fellow Israelites had met with an immediate positive response. All sorts of men with little or no battle training had rallied around him. They had risen to meet his blood-stirring challenges. Ferociously that day they had flung themselves into combat. They came from his own clan, from Asher, Naphtali, all of Manasseh, and even Ephraim. But when Gideon asked no more than a bit of bread and drink from Succoth, then later Penuel, he was derided for even daring to do so.

Almost in derision they taunted him. "Have you come with the hands of Zebah and Zalmunna in yours? Why you haven't even overtaken these fierce warriors. Yet you ask us to supply you with bread as though you were already victorious."

It was a two-pronged put-down. First of all, it paid indirect homage to the prowess of the wild desert chieftains who had pillaged Palestine for seven dreadful years. Second, it was a slur and insult to the gallantry of Gideon.

Beyond both of these, however, was the indisputable fact that the residents of both Succoth and Penuel had no confidence at all in the God of Israel. Long since, they had deliberately separated themselves from their fellow countrymen. With calculating intent they had moved into enemy territory across the Jordan. And there in a double-minded way, they lived uneasily in the wilderness with divided loyalties and affections.

They were really neither Israelites nor bedouin. They were neither truly among God's own chosen people, nor really allied wholeheartedly with their fierce adversaries. They were neither really hot nor cold. Like shriveled stalks of sun-bleached grass, they bent to the winds of circumstance, no matter which way they blew. They were forever trying to play it safe and cozy to accommodate themselves.

For a man with the tremendous thrust of Gideon, such softness and pussyfooting was nauseating. He could not stomach such duplicity and indecision. His response to Succoth's syrupy stand was that when he returned from the desert in victory, he would have to discipline this community with startling severity. Likewise to Penuel he made it very clear that the strong tower in which their confidence reposed would be razed, leaving them vulnerable. It was a tough lesson they would need to be taught. Their strength lay not in man-made structures of stone, bricks, or beams but in Jehovah God.

Gideon's ferocious treatment of these "halfway" people was not to be some personal vindictive action. He was not a "little man" out to even the score with those who scorned him. He was not just getting back at those who belittled him. He simply saw himself as an instrument of justice and judgment in the hands of Jehovah God. He was just as willing to be the one used to "cut down" and tear away the duplicity and double-dealing of these disloyal Israelites as he had been to tear down and demolish the altar and grove of the false gods in Israel.

It would be harsh treatment that Succoth and Penuel would receive. Gideon did not indulge himself with mere idle threats. He was a man of action. What he said, he did. He may have had other weaknesses in his makeup, but indecision was not one of them. He had met God. He had seen God move in majestic power on his behalf. So there was no stopping him now in his advance against the enemy.

Unless one has lived in these Middle Eastern countries and is familiar with their culture, many of the incidents recounted in the history of Israel may seem to us terribly crude and cruel. Unfortunately very often the ruthless treatment and spine-chilling atrocities carried out have been misconstrued as coming from divine edict. This simply is not so. Just as in the case of modern warfare where masses of innocent victims have suffered under atomic bombs, incendiary bombs, napalm bombs, and even gas or germ warfare, no one can say these lethal weapons are of God's design. They are the product of a perverted humanity which refuses to accept or acknowledge the rule and conduct of a righteous God.

There is inherent in the basic ongoing of the cosmos

certain irrevocable principles. These have been God ordained. And anyone who contravenes them does so at his
own enormous peril. This explains why human societies
which deliberately ignore or spurn the righteousness of a
gracious God are so merciless and cruel.

In Gideon's day—and even in our times in some Mus-
lim countries—it was not uncommon to cut off a man's
hands if he was found stealing. For the remainder of his
wretched life, the poor victim would be compelled to beg
for a living. His severed stumps would be an enduring
reminder both to him and his community that there was
an appalling penalty to pay for thievery. By the same measure a woman taken in adultery was smashed to a pulp by
her neighbors outside the village walls. Women just did
not dare to indulge in illicit sexual relationships. A man
who committed rape was thrust through with spears and
swords. His blood was spilt in the main town square
where it stained the stones. Its black and almost indelible
stain was a grim reminder to any would-be rapist that
such activity could cost him his life. And for disloyalty to
his people in time of war, a man's back could be torn and
lacerated using the cruel thorn branches of the desert
acacia for a lash.

These fierce and fearsome forms of brutality were
woven into the warp and woof of their ferocious lives. We
need to remind ourselves that the ongoing history of the
human family has been a story stained by blood and carnage. Yet into this appalling picture of suffering comes
the compassion and concern of our God who cares deeply
for the awful dilemma of His earth children. Always He is
endeavoring in any way possible, to turn us from the
perverseness of our paths and the wickedness of our
ways. He sends His own appointed servants to discipline,

direct, and draw us back to His precepts. Those He loves and cares about, He disciplines.

In God's great, good hand, Gideon was to become a scourge to Succoth and Penuel. He was the one chosen to correct their wrongdoing. It was he who would have to bear the brunt of the blame for bearing down on them so hard when he returned from battle.

Succoth and Penuel were both places which had special significance for Israel. They were not just nondescript villages out in the wilderness. Rather, they were tied in strongly to the very ancient traditions of this nation. It was at Penuel where Jacob had met and wrestled with the angel of the Lord. It was there, alone, in the darkness of that fierce contest that Jacob, the "supplanter," became known as Israel, "a prince with God." He who had been such a double-dealer had at last come clean to become a champion and patriarch of his people. The men of Penuel knew this. It was a heroic tradition with them. Yet here they themselves had slipped back into the ignominious traits of their traditional hero.

Succoth was almost as much at fault. It was called "the place of the booths," in memory of the fact that here Jacob (Israel) had made camp with his family just before meeting Esau. His reconciliation with his brother whom he had so grievously defrauded of his birthright had been a masterstroke of statesmanship.

So both Succoth and Penuel were places with a proud and noble tradition. But tradition itself was not enough to preserve a people from peril. They were communities with a great name, but those names had come to be "*no name*" because of their compromise. All of this, Gideon, as God's man of the hour, was determined to correct. But first there was one more battle to be fought and a final conquest to be consummated.

Relentlessly Gideon pushed on out into the terrible heat and blazing sun of the Transjordan deserts. Only a general of enormous charisma and command would be followed by his band of three hundred into such horrendous hardship.

Here daytime temperatures hover around 120 degrees. The heat is appalling, burning, scorching, shriveling men in its terrible intensity. Heat waves shimmer above the hot stones and sand. The brilliant, ghastly, intense sunlight sears the eyeballs, scorches the skin, desiccates the body with its brutal burning. The best of men are benumbed by the awesome torment of terrible thirst and grim lassitude that grips them as in a vicious vise.

But Gideon would not give way. He pushed on relentlessly. With a stroke of great genius, he led his men in a wide circle far out to the east of Karkor. This outpost of the enemy is where Zebah and Zalmunna had encamped after their escape across the Jordan.

Their old, cocky self-confidence had come back to the two desert chiefs. They were so sure of themselves in these dry desert wastes. Here they were on home territory. Here they had the distinct advantage of familiarity with this formidable terrain. Settling in comfortably with their remaining forces of some fifteen thousand fighters, they were sure no Israelite would ever dare to attack them in this stronghold.

They really did not know Gideon. They had underrated the unshakable courage of this young commander. They were to be taken by utter surprise a second time. Their attacker would come at them from a totally unexpected quarter—from the eastern desert.

Again the odds against Gideon were overwhelming.

Here he was with a small, tired, hungry band of three hundred thirsty men attacking a force of fifteen thousand desert warriors. Yet he and his men were inflamed with victory. They were thirsting for one last mighty triumph. Even if the odds against them were fifty to one, they would win. God was with them. The Lord Jehovah was their King.

Sweeping down on Karkor from the east, Gideon cut the enemy host to shreds before they could collect themselves from their comfortable composure. The Israelites were fierce as desert falcons stooping to the kill. That day Karkor lived up to its name *"the place of battering down."* There God granted Gideon his second great conquest. There Gideon again lived up to his name "the cutter down." It was an hour of great glory.

The Midianites fled and scattered. They were driven hither and thither like dust before the wind. Overwhelmed with terror, they were slaughtered in their tracks. Their bodies littered the dry ridges and dongas. By night jackals would scavange their carcasses; by day the vultures would pick their bones; and for forty years their fierce war shouts would be stilled across the wastes.

Zebah, "the sacrifice," and his comrade in arms, Zalmunna "no shade or shelter," tried to escape but were captured in midflight. It was a tremendous exploit for Gideon's men. Their victims would know what it was to taste the sword; to see themselves as human sacrifices; to know there was no place to turn now for shade or shelter from the fierceness of their formidable foe.

For Gideon this was the moment of ultimate triumph. This was the moment of truth. This was the final confirmation of God's word to him in Ophrah, under the old, gnarled oak: "I will be with thee and smite the Midianites as one man."

But for Gideon there was much more than the vindication of his faith in the Lord—great as that had been. There was here also the enormous double blessing of discovering that his God, Jehovah, was also the God of rich and wondrous compensation to His people.

He had been so willing to give honor and precedent to Ephraim for capturing Oreb and Zeeb earlier in the battle. Now there had fallen into his own hands Zebah and Zalmunna, equally notorious desert hawks. This was as great an accolade as any he had bestowed on his comrades in arms. So there he stood now, supreme in his prestige as the outright, undisputed leader of his nation.

This is ever the way with God. He honors those who honor Him. He is ever active in raising up to great heights those who humbly walk with Him. He is the Lord God not only of all consolation but also the God of all compensation. It is He who lifts one man up and sets another down. It is He who guarantees that the last shall be first and the first shall be last. These were and are eternal principles that He has determined should function in the affairs of men. And it is a wise and prudent person who walks humbly before Him, reveling quietly in His divine companionship.

With this great battle behind them, Gideon and his now illustrious three hundred took a break. It was time to slake their thirst, assuage their hunger, and refresh their weary bodies. There are few records in history anywhere of so few valiant warriors having conquered so many of the enemy with so little equipment.

When they returned from the eastern desert, it was by way of the high rugged mountain pass of Heres. In our idiom this would be known as "the pass of the sun." In

their triumphal train marched the two shackled warrior
chieftains. They were the supreme trophies of war whom
Gideon brought back as final and irrefutable proof of his
conquests under God. It was no woebegone band of men
who marched with him. Rather they were troops flushed
with victory and the honor of their God.

11

Gideon's Discipline

On the way back to the Jordan and their homes to the west of it, Gideon's men captured a young man from Succoth. This turned out to be a remarkable windfall. It was not just happenstance or coincidence. Like so many of the amazing things which had taken place with lightninglike rapidity in his meteoric career, it was arranged and ordained of God.

This youthful captive was no nondescript castoff from the community of Succoth. Quite the reverse, he was one of the key people there. With his extensive knowledge of all its inhabitants, he was able to describe to Gideon in minute and exact detail the names and residences of all seventy-seven of the community leaders.

This inside information that fell into Gideon's hands was precisely what he needed. It would enable him to sort out the princes, leaders, and other hierarchy of Succoth who had so blatantly refused him supplies. Undoubtedly there would have been some of the common people who might have given his armed men food and refreshment to carry them to battle with the enemy. But it was their leaders who had taunted Gideon to provide them with tangible proof that he would ultimately be the victor.

These seventy-seven men were the moving force who influenced all their people to have *no faith* either in Gideon's cause or in the Lord God of Israel. That this could be so is all the more amazing when one stops to consider that some 120,000 of the Midianite forces had been slain in battle before even Gideon came to Succoth.

Now Gideon had all the precise data needed to execute fair and appropriate discipline on this maverick community. The exact list of the leaders must have come as a terrifying shock to Succoth. It was a first knockout blow of special, well-nigh superspiritual insight which stunned the whole community. Well may they have asked: "Where did this man obtain such information with such rapidity? Wasn't he away in combat? Did he leave spies planted among us?" These and a score of other searching questions must have swept through the dusty village streets. Gideon had come back to scourge them precisely as he had promised to do. Here was no man of mere empty threats.

What happened to Gideon in this instance is indicative of what very often takes place in the lives of those who really do God's will. I often refer to them as "God's bonuses." The Lord makes available to those who walk humbly with Him, enormous insights, or otherwise unexplainable advantages which would not otherwise be theirs. He provides guidance, direction and data ordinarily beyond one's ability to gather or possess. He puts them in positions of enormous advantage. He arranges and coordinates the events of their lives in unique and wonderful ways.

It is this element of seeing God's hand at work that lends such a keen sense of wonder and excitement to a Christian's career. There are no accidents in his activities. He senses with an acute awareness that the Lord is very much at work behind the amazing sequence of his affairs. And in this he not only finds great confidence but also enormous adventure in his companionship with God.

This experience is not something unique or restricted only to outstanding men and women of God. It can be and often is the daily delight of those whose simple trust is in the Lord.

As Gideon's men rounded up the seventy-seven shaken leaders of Succoth, they were fully aware that their discipline would be God directed. This was not a case of Gideon evening the score for their previous insults to him. It was not a question of taking vengeance or venting his spleen. Nor was it even a matter of getting mad and abusing his indifferent "brethren" for their cruel callousness to his cause.

What Succoth was to be taught on this terrible day was the high cost of riding the fence. They were to see what price one paid for belittling God and ridiculing His ability to deliver His own people. They were to learn the agonizing lesson that to be lukewarm was something abhorrent and despicable.

Gideon ordered the two shackled desert princes, Zebah and Zalmunna, to step forward before all the villagers. Standing there stripped of their regalia, no longer mounted on their caparisoned camels, disheveled and bloodstained, the two princes appeared more like a couple of scarecrows than haughty desert chiefs.

"Here are the prizes you taunted me about," Gideon shouted to the trembling crowd, now cowed with fear.

"You flung the taunt in my face, when I came to you seeking supplies for my men, that Zebah and Zalmunna were not yet in my hand." His eyes smoldered and his voice thundered in terrifying solemnity. "Here they are; see for yourselves. God has given both them, and the names of your notorious leaders, into my power."

It would almost be best to draw down a veil over the excruciating details of the appalling lashing then measured out to the men of Succoth. It was a scene repeatedly played out in the cruel life of the cruel Middle East.

The victims were forced to lie facedown in the dust of their own village streets. Their clothing was stripped away rudely to lay bare their bodies. Then strong men thrashed them unmercifully with the rough branches of the desert acacias or other scrub thorn. The talons on these branches were sharpened rapiers that tore through flesh and tissue with agonizing pain. Blood and humor gushed from the gaping wounds. It was a ghastly flogging, sometimes consummated by dragging the hapless victims across the rough ground until their skin was shredded from their bodies in excruciating torture.

Leaving Succoth to groan in its agony, Gideon and his forces pushed on to Penuel. Perhaps word of their impending punishment sped before the advancing general. Again Gideon was to demonstrate that he was a man of his word. Even though flushed with victory and exuberant with his conquests, he was not about to forget the formidable decree made to these proud people of Penuel. Perhaps they felt impregnable in their desert fort with its high walls and impressive lookout tower. Maybe they thought they could make light of a man whose trust was in God, who claimed that it was Jehovah God who would grant him great victory, and they chided and scoffed at his childlike confidence in the Lord.

Soon they discovered how suddenly the tables of their lives could be turned when God was in the setting. Men do not make light either of God or His people with impunity. There ultimately comes an hour of reckoning. There comes a time of truth. There comes a settling of the score. It has always been thus. It will ever be so. Puny men do not lampoon the Almighty without paying an appalling price for their insolence. It matters not whether it be in the case of individuals or nations.

So Gideon's forces assaulted and tore down the fortress tower of Penuel. As the walls and parapets of sun-dried bricks and desert stone came crashing to the ground, the occupants poured out like ants scurrying from their anthill. But their frenzied flight was too late. Their panic did not preserve them. They were put to the sword by Gideon's fierce three hundred.

When the siege and slaughter were over, Gideon marched away leaving behind a broken town. Its walled fortress flattened; its men dead; its strength shattered; this proud arrogant village lay open and vulnerable to every raider who passed by. In fact it would become to all who traversed these desert wastes a byword of the severity of Gideon's ferocious discipline. Even Zebah and Zalmunna looked on askance, and their own fierce hearts turned to terror.

In the tradition of his times, Gideon returned home to Abiezer with the triumphal panoply of a splendid warlord. In his train came the once-fierce Midianite princes, Zebah and Zalmunna. Besides them there would be a whole host of captive prisoners, young men, pretty girls, and others who would become slaves and servants. As well, there would be caravans of camels bearing booty and loot of every sort stripped from the fallen enemy forces.

It was all a part of the cruel business of war. It was the culmination of gory battles and great gallantry. It was the ending to a triumphant engagement.

As the conquering heroes came marching home, people would come tumbling out of their homes and villages to sing and shout their adulation. Children would clap their hands and chant praises in gleeful excitement. Farmers would pause in their fields to wave happily with relief. There was jubilation everywhere. The long enemy occupation was over. The Midianite invaders had been overthrown and crushed. Gideon was their national idol. The hero was home!

It was probably this public applause, more than any other thing, which began to be Gideon's undoing. Like most men, he would have some difficulty handling success. It seemed to go to his head a bit.

Not until he had reached his little familiar farmstead at Ophrah did he start to question and interrogate his two captive chiefs. Rumor had it that they were in fact the very ones who had killed his older brothers at Tabor. When pressed closely on this point both Zebah and Zalmunna admitted to committing terrible atrocities there.

In an attempt to curry favor with Gideon, hoping that perchance he might spare their lives, they resorted to flattery. "In fact those we slaughtered were veritable princes," they smiled slyly, oiling their slippery words with characteristic Eastern subtlety. "They resembled you, Gideon, sons of a king!"

Of course, in one sense Gideon may have felt genuinely flattered by so lofty a compliment. To a degree it was well deserved. He had conducted himself in battle like royalty.

He had commanded his men with consummate skill and courage. He was in truth a prince of a man in his own right. He had earned this accolade from his enemies with élan.

But Gideon was not about to be bamboozled by such cunning. He was no fool. He was a down-to-earth farm fellow who knew very well where his roots and heritage lay. He came from one of the least-respected tribes of Israel. His father's clan was one of the least impressive even though Joash bore a proud name among his people. And all of them together, he and his brothers, were but humble countrymen, struggling to survive on their sparse and marginal properties. But "princes," no, not princes! Just plain people who had been brutally plundered and pillaged by these merciless Midianites.

Despite the tremendous triumphs of the past few days; despite the incredible victories granted by God; despite the aura of honor and glory in which he now moved, Gideon had not forgotten the grim, grinding, ghastly years underground. He remembered very clearly and very vividly the atrocities perpetrated under the cruel heel of the Midianites. He recalled the calamity, suffering, and sorrow in his family when news came to his home that his own brothers had been brutally massacred by the ruthless desert raiders now standing in chains before him. There were sly smirks on their faces, and it made his blood boil. Their blood would be spilt for his brothers' blood.

To Gideon's credit it must be conceded that even in this, his hour of power, he was given to greatness and to generosity. His reply to Zebah and Zalmunna is startling in its striking sincerity. "If you had spared my brothers, the sons of my mother, whose heart you shattered, I would spare you." A look of pathos crossed his strong face. "But because you did not, your blood must be spilled for theirs" (*see* Genesis 9:6).

This edict was God's, not Gideon's. It had been so foreordained from the earliest era of his ancestors under God's direction. In taking the lives of these two men he was complying with what had been commanded from time immemorial. But there was more to it than just that. It is important to recognize a powerful principle here. The slaying of the two desert warriors now in his hand was not cold-blooded revenge for himself. It was an act of justice and retribution on behalf of his father and his mother, who had suffered the loss of their sons. Also it was a settlement of the score on behalf of his brothers' families left destitute and distraught by their deaths.

Gideon then did a very peculiar thing—perhaps a very cruel thing, certainly a very unbecoming thing. He ordered his oldest son, a mere stripling lad, a gangling, awkward boy in his early teens, to thrust the desert princes through with his sword. It was asking too much of the youngster. Even if he was the son of a now-famous father, this was an act beyond his ability.

The two proud princes also sensed that this was a crude gesture below the character of Gideon. A man of his caliber did not add insult to injury. They were prepared to die. But if die they must, at least it should be with dignity, beneath the fierce sword of a great and gallant fighting man.

Gideon saw his mistake. Without a moment's delay or hesitation, he hurled himself at the two captives and cut them to the ground. It was the climax to his campaign. He had been the first to raise the sword to overthrow the oppressor, now he was the last to sheath it. For forty years

now he would never again need to draw it from its scab-
bard.

With a last, final flourish Gideon had the golden ornaments and chains stripped from the camels of his captives. It was a signal to all his followers that they could
follow suit. The war was over. The spoils were theirs.
They deserved recompense for their bravery. This was
their grand finale!

12

Gideon and His Gold

Tremendous excitement, commingled with exuberant enthusiasm, swept across Israel. In the matter of a few desperate days of battle this nation had undergone an incredible metamorphosis. Emerging from the constricting bondage and darkness of their subterranean existence, they burst into a new life of glittering gaiety like a full-formed butterfly breaking out of its cryptlike cocoon.

Israel, the nation under God, quite literally did want to try her wings. She felt she was in a position now not only to have shed the shackles of the enemy, but even to step free and clear of the constrictions of their theocracy under God.

It was really a case of being a bit drunk with power. The glory of victory and ecstasy of conquest was a heady mixture that most of these downtrodden people could not handle very well. It went to their heads. And, as is so often the case, they were carried away from the facts of reality in their frenzy.

It was the Lord God, Jehovah, who had been with them

in battle. It was He who had made good on His commitment to Gideon that He would deliver Israel from her dilemma. It was He who had discomfitted the overwhelming armies of the Midianites. It was He who had given Gideon the encouragement, leadership, and expertise to execute amazing military strategy. It was He who had provided the energy and inspiration needed for a tiny handful of men to rout and overcome a huge enemy force of overwhelming superiority.

Essentially the battle had been the Lord's. He was the victor. But in the glory of that triumph, Israel's attention was focused not on God, but on Gideon. It was in him that they saw their hero, their hope, their possible first king.

Their attention had been diverted from the God of their salvation to a mere man. For all of Israel this was a dangerous digression. It might well have led to terrible results and devastating consequences. Fortunately for them Gideon did not succumb to their mass hysteria.

People so often behave like sheep. They move under the impulse of a strange, powerful mob instinct. In a moment the masses can be gripped with a mania. This is an inherent weakness in human society which individuals, hungry for power and obsessed with ambition, can manipulate and exploit to their own selfish advantage.

Had Gideon so desired in this his hour of triumph, he could have seized the sovereignty of his people. They would gladly, readily, have rewarded him with royal acclaim. They would happily have made him their first monarch. He would have been acclaimed their king. He could have established a regal dynasty beginning with himself, carried on through his stripling son Jether, and eventually on through his grandsons.

It would have been a most alluring prospect for most men. To be granted such enormous power and prestige by one's people was a glittering prospect which lesser men would have grabbed—but not Gideon.

His response to this suggestion gives us a remarkable insight into the character of the man. Vehemently he protested: "I shall not rule over you, neither shall my son rule over you: the Lord shall rule over you!"

It was a simple, straightforward declaration of incredible magnitude. It reveals the genuine humility of the man. He was unassuming, and yet at the same time, very wise. Obviously success had not gone to his head. He had retained a calm, collected view of himself and his own inabilities. He had sufficient spiritual maturity to recognize that it was the Lord God who had granted victory to Israel. He still saw the strategy and superior role played by Jehovah in the life of this nation. And on this account Gideon insisted that honor be given to whom honor was due.

Had the historical record of Gideon concluded at this point, he would stand securely as one of the most remarkable men in the annals of Israel. But his story did not end there. Like so many human narratives, it goes on to disclose that as with all of us, Gideon, too, had an Achilles' heel in his makeup.

A remarkable aspect of the scriptural accounts of men and women with whom God deals is their utter authenticity. There is never any attempt made to whitewash people. No glossing over of a character is allowed. We see them shown to us in their true colors. It matters not whether it be Moses, David, Hezekiah, or Gideon; they are not portrayed as perfect people living like gilded birds in golden cages. Rather we see them struggling in the lights and shadows of their own unique makeup, striving against the assaults of sin and selfishness which all of us face in life.

So as we look now on this magnificent young man, we sense a sinister shadow stealing across the scene. It is as though his great and noble triumph would be tarnished by tragedy that had its source in his one great weakness—gold! He had not been allured or drawn away by the glitter of kingship. But when it came to gold—the raw, bare, precious element—something deep within his makeup was ignited. An enormous, overpowering desire for sudden wealth, sudden security, sudden spending power engulfed Gideon.

He looked on the spoils of war gathered up by his men, and it mesmerized his gaze. He, the poor land farmer from Ophrah, had never ever seen such wealth. The booty stripped from the Midianites was almost unbelievable. There were gorgeous golden earrings, exquisite necklaces, golden camel chains, Ishmaelite ornaments of all sorts, besides royal purple robes, elaborately embellished with gold thread, and other lavish trappings common to the fierce camel warriors.

What Gideon saw, he wanted. And he wanted it in very large measure. In fact he demanded it of every man. There was burning in his bones, a covetous craving for every gold earring he could lay his hands on.

Surprisingly enough his wish was granted. The prompt response and immediate reaction of his men was to fling one of the gorgeous royal gowns on the ground. Into it every man tossed the golden earrings and ornaments stripped from the fallen foe.

Again a sort of mass hysteria swept through Gideon's forces. In glee and jubilant gaiety they watched the glitter-

ing mound of jewelry pile up in a mounting pyramid
under the summer sun. Light flashed and sparkled from a
thousand polished surfaces as the earrings and necklaces
tumbled on top of one another.

It is especially surprising that not a single soldier
stopped to ask his commander what would be done with
the gold. Not one warrior even questioned the reason
behind this otherwise unreasonable demand. In war and
victory every man was entitled to his share of the spoils.
Who or what did Gideon have in mind?

If we pause to calculate roughly what the value of this
accumulated gold was worth, it will astonish us. The
weight collected was 1,700 shekels of gold. Translated into
our troy weights, this is seventy pounds. At the current
price of gold on the world markets, its equivalent value in
today's currency would be in the neighborhood of
$134,000. In addition to this amount of gold in earrings
alone, Gideon was given gorgeous chains, neck ornaments, and royal robes of immeasurable worth.

It can be assumed that the total value of all his acquisi-
tions that day easily exceeded a quarter of a million dol-
lars. It was a straightforward case of instant riches. The
dust-bowl farmer had suddenly found himself a fortune.
And unfortunately it was to become his folly.

Gideon was by no means the first, nor the last of his
race, to have problems with the yellow metal. Gold,
though such a precious commodity, bears with it its own
peculiar burden of bondage. It offers such liberty, yet so
often leads its owner into the prison of his own posses-
siveness. It has the capacity to subvert with appalling
consequences those who pursue it.

Gideon's forefathers, under the indiscretion of Aaron,
had flung their gold at Aaron's feet to have it fashioned

into a golden calf. Around this false image, they danced and feasted until Moses came storming down off the smoking, rumbling mount of God. Israel's incredible folly brought them within a hairbreadth of utter annihilation beneath the hand of the Lord whom they had so grossly spurned.

Again after the battle of Jericho, Achan had seen and coveted enemy gold and garments. He hid the forbidden booty in a pit dug beneath the floor of his tent. This covert act of direct disobedience led to the discomfiture of Joshua's armies when they assaulted Ai. It was a terrible rout for Israel. Dismayed and discouraged Joshua flung himself on his face upon the ground before the Lord. What had gone wrong? It was the glitter of gold that had undone the armies of Israel.

The magnetism of materialism is insidious and devastating. In the retinue of great kings who would ultimately follow long after Gideon, gold was to become a terrible trap. Even Solomon, with all his wisdom granted from God, could not keep from being subverted by gold. It brought him foreign wives and concubines who led his heart astray to follow false gods.

Hezekiah, one of the most outstanding leaders ever to arise in Jerusalem, met his nemesis in gold. It inflamed his heart, pandered to his pride, and induced him to display his wealth to the Babylonians. Alternately they, too, were gripped with gold fever. They came marching against Jerusalem, stripped both Hezekiah and the gorgeous temple of its gold, then took Israel away into captivity.

Gideon's handling of gold may have been well intentioned, yet it was essentially badly mistaken. We are not given the exact details of all that he did with his hoard.

Just the bare bones remain in the historical record to remind us that the best of men can be subverted by sudden wealth.

He instructed that a gorgeous golden ephod be made. An ephod was the special tunic reserved exclusively for the use of the high priest who served God on behalf of his people. As he ministered before the altar in the Tabernacle, he wore this gorgeous garment of gleaming blue brocade. It had attached to its shoulder straps the names of the twelve tribes of Israel. As the high priest ministered before God, interceding for his nation, he bore ever before the Ark of the Lord the names of his people.

During this period in Israel's history, the home of the Ark, the Tabernacle, and the chief high priest was in Shiloh. This was a small village not far from Jerusalem in Judah. And it was there, and only there, that the high priest could minister on behalf of all his people before the Lord.

Gideon knew this and so did his family and friends. Yet somehow the gold now in his possession induced him to do this very naive and foolish thing. It may well be argued that Gideon was endeavoring to try to turn the attention of his people back to Jehovah. It may have been that the true Levitical priesthood of his time was terribly decadent. It was no doubt his burning desire to see a new impulse and impetus in the spiritual life of Israel that led him to have the golden ephod put on display in his home town of Ophrah.

Still none of these reasons truly exonerated his decision. For though he had been the one who here demolished the power of the false gods of Baal and Ashtaroth, he was really now putting another false idol in their place.

Put very bluntly, Gideon was simply substituting one form of false worship with another. He had fallen into the trap of taking away one idol only to put another in its place. This would have been serious enough had it only involved his own immediate family. The tragedy was it enmeshed all of his nation. The whole of Israel went astray.

The responsibility of moral or spiritual leadership is an enormous burden for any man to bear. It takes a continuous ongoing, undeviating devotion to the Lord to lead others aright. One of the formidable temptations ever present in Christian work is to have our attention focused upon that which we ourselves have produced or taken upon ourselves in false honor.

Gideon fashioned an ephod of gold, and it became a snare to him, his family, his friends, and his entire nation. It captivated their attention. It took them away from focusing their faith on the Lord God, Jehovah. To us, looking on from afar, this may appear foolish and absurd. Yet all too often we are snared in a similar diversion.

In Christian circles it is not at all uncommon for a church or group of believers to be completely caught up with the contemporary concepts of their activity or life. Some groups literally idolize their leaders because of pleasing personalities, special charisma, or outstanding gifts and abilities. Others are totally enamored with the actual structure of their church or society. It may be some magnificent edifice of stone, steel, glass, or timber. Alternatively it might be the program of the organization, its budget, or its elaborate machinery for producing remarkable statistics. No matter what it is, as long as it appears to spell s-u-c-c-e-s-s, people will succumb to its allure. In so doing very often the Lord God who granted the success is relegated to second place.

This essentially became Gideon's downfall. The golden ephod stood as a constant reminder of his own glittering achievements. It dimmed his clear view and memory of the Lord who had met him under the oak when all he owned was a small kid and one bare bucket of grain.

13

Gideon's Twilight Years

IN SPITE OF THE DISTRACTION caused by Gideon's golden ephod, he himself remained a remarkable force in Israel for the next forty years. It is indeed a measure of the man that without either pretense or ostentation his strong quiet presence among his people provided a base for peace. He had no need to take power into his hands nor assume undue authority over his contemporaries. Just being there was a guarantee of his great and godly influence in Israel.

The overthrow and defeat of Midian had been so complete and so final that never again did they pose even a threat from beyond the Jordan. Not even a remote remnant remained to raise its head again like a desert adder, wounded yet ready to strike. Gideon's unrelenting pursuit into the far reaches and desert wastes of the Midianite domain had spelled out their final decimation. Not only had Gideon's vicious victory stilled Midian, but it stood as a grim and awesome warning to any other would-be aggressor who might have had designs on Israel.

All the enemy nations round about were well aware that the regal lion of Israel was quietly ensconced in Ophrah. He dared not be disturbed in his den. If he ever was, he would come roaring out again to defend Israel from her adversary. The net result was that this peculiar people under God, though saved from direct attack from without, gradually began to undergo moral decay from within. Amid their peace and quiet the insidious forces of spiritual degeneration and moral degradation did their deadly work.

It is a strange phenomenon in human society that very often in serene situations, the most dangerous seeds of retrogression are sown. Sated with peace and prosperity, people seem to become suitable seedbeds for the most insidious sorts of softness and sensual preoccupation. It is akin to noxious weeds spreading through the whole wide field of society. Men are literally smothered by sin without a complaint, and ruined by the influence of corruption on every side.

To a degree what was happening to all of Israel as a nation was also in truth happening to Gideon as an individual. We are given a rather detailed account of his main preoccupation during the twilight years of his life. What we see is a microcosm of the whole pageantry of his people.

Gideon had been content merely to return to his home in Ophrah. Of course he came back a much more wealthy man than when he went away. With his new-found riches he was in a position to acquire numerous wives and concubines. And from these marriages there were born to him some seventy sons. He became, in fact, a formidable patriarch in Israel. We are given the impression that Gideon's twilight years were tranquil and serene. He lived to the ripe old age, for his time, of about seventy years. His days were always surrounded with the delight of much domestic activity. He was quite obviously a hero not only to his children and grandchildren, but also to the friends and neighbors of his community.

No doubt Gideon's home in Ophrah was more or less the hub of activity for Israel as a people. They looked to this great patriarch as their judge, their leader, and their saviour. No details are given as to what roles of responsibility Gideon was willing to assume after his great victory over the Midianites. But it must be assumed he was a man of enormous influence for good in all of Israel because of his implicit trust in the Lord.

At last the day came, when in great dignity and honor, he was buried in the mausoleum of Joash, his father. It marked the end of an era. It was as if sealing this sepulcher was closing the door on a glorious chapter in the annals of Israel. Gideon's influence for good and for God; his majestic magnetism and unique charisma; his leadership and uplift for his wayward people all were buried with him.

Most melancholy of all, his devotion to God and his faith in the Lord Jehovah of his forefathers was a facet of his life that seemed to have failed to make any enduring impact on Israel. When Gideon was gone, these, too, were gone, buried as it were in the darkness of his own death. No restraining spiritual light or illumination remained to light the path of a people who were determined to plunge back into the blackness of Baal and Ashtaroth.

No sooner had Gideon gone underground than all of Israel forgot not only him but also his God. It was as if he almost had never been on the center stage of this strange nation's sad and painful story. Few are the races of the earth who have given rise to greater geniuses than has Israel. Her story is replete, even down to this very day, with brilliant men and women of enormous gifts and unparalleled abilities. Though a race relatively small in numbers, scattered all across the earth among the nations of the world, Israel has produced more than her share of inspiring people and impressive individuals. Yet her history is full of tragic heroes.

Gideon was one of these. Gideon was a man who in his finest hour brought great glory not only to himself, his family, and his nation, but also to his God. But by the same measure he was also a man who in his weaker moments perpetrated great folly not only for himself but also for those who followed him.

He leaves us with a classic, clear-cut picture of one who knew what it was to walk humbly with his God in greatness. He leaves us also with the solemn, sobering view of a man who missed the mark when his personal preferences overruled God's gracious will for his life.

14

A Call to Action

THE EXPLOITS OF GIDEON have been recorded for us in God's Word with authenticity and authority. They are more than the mere report of a most remarkable life under the direct guidance of God. Stimulating and inspiring as such biographical sketches may be, they demand more than our enjoyment of them.

Implicit in this narrative of a man "given to God" is the inescapable compulsion that calls us to action. There is no reason why in the latter half of the twentieth century, God's Spirit should not call some of us to become equally great men and women of valor.

The simple, penetrating truth is that God in Christ, by His gracious Spirit, does come to us just as surely as He came to Gideon under the tough, old oak in Ophrah. He does commune with us. He does challenge us to great exploits. He does call us to bold action in implicit obedience. He does promise us His presence, His power, His perseverance to accomplish the "impossible" in our tempestuous times.

The simple question is: "Will I respond in a positive way, empowered by Him, to do promptly the thing He instructs me to do?" If so, then titanic events will take place both in my own life, and in the world around me.

Definite steps embracing profound principles that lead
in that direction can be seen in the pages that follow.

You the reader, can become a modern-day Gideon
under God's great hand. You can be one to accomplish
giant feats for the Lord during your life. I here present in
precise form the salient truths demonstrated to us in the
history of God's dealing with Gideon. This will serve both
as a reminder and résumé of all that has here been written
before.

1. Any nation, community, family, or person that
   compromises with evil faces ultimate catastrophe.
2. The laws of God, designed for the well-being of
   men, if ignored, prove inexorable. They eventually
   crush those who contravene them.
3. Sinning always leads eventually, not to laughter
   and gaiety, but to horrendous suffering.
4. Strange as it may seem, most men will not cry out to
   God for deliverance until crushed. Out of despair
   comes the call for help.
5. Because God is so gracious, so generous, so
   greathearted, He never does turn a deaf ear, even to
   chronic offenders.
6. He is more anxious to deliver us from our dilemmas
   than we are. Somehow most of us love the slime pit
   of sin.
7. The disciplines of hardship and disaster are really a
   demonstration of the Lord's deep love for His own.
8. Amid the darkness and despair of those mired in
   evil, He comes to help anyone who will respond.
9. He is unable to rescue those who refuse to be re-
   stored. If a man is to know God's strength, he must
   respond to it.

10. God's great purposes for His people are, more often than not, accomplished through the instrumentality of one man or woman.

11. The Lord's relationship to us is a very private, personal one. It is based upon an individual's availability to God, not upon any special gift or genius.

12. It matters not how unpromising the person or place may appear from a human perspective; God can see the potential.

13. He takes the most unlikely individual to achieve the most remarkable results.

14. The key to such success lies in the implicit compliance of a man with God's will.

15. This sort of obedience and prompt cooperation comes at great cost. It entails setting aside one's own wishes.

16. It is self-sacrifice of this caliber which frees God's great hand to move mightily in a man's life. He no longer ties God's hands nor restricts His Spirit.

17. With humble, open, available people the Lord delights to dwell. They are His favorite friends.

18. It is His presence which provides the strength, stability, and serenity needed for great achievements.

19. It is this living presence of God's Spirit within who produces peace. He provides the needed guidance and direction for all decisions.

20. The individual, who then proceeds to do simply what is asked of him, will discover enormous power with God.

21. It is God Himself who energizes and enables a mere man to accomplish enormous exploits.

22. This has far-reaching influence on a person's fam-

ily, friends, neighbors, community, and nation. It is a contagion.

23. Others will often rally to the call of a person whose life is centered in God and not self-centered.

24. There is an inherent need among most men for spiritual leadership. They look for it. They gravitate to it when it can be found.

25. The accomplishment of God's purposes on this planet is not dependent on large-scale operations. His economy is based not on man's measurements but on divine dynamics.

26. One man with God can be a majority in any situation.

27. Despite what we may appear to observe around us, the Lord is actively and energetically at work behind the scenes.

28. The ongoing enterprises of God's Spirit are eternal. In the end they ultimately prevail despite all that is contrary.

29. It is the wise person who aligns himself in harmony with the will of God for the world. To do otherwise is to invite inevitable disaster.

30. For the person who seeks and does God's will there are glorious compensations and exciting conquests.

31. Victory comes at a high cost. That price is the willingness to be seen as a fool for God.

32. The Lord is ever faithful to those who follow Him. He never double-deals anyone who is loyal. He honors them.

33. The awareness of God's special touch upon one's life brings to it special dignity and direction.

34. The presence of God's own gracious Spirit injects patience and perseverance into a man's performance. He is energized with amazing endurance.

35. Similarly the person who walks humbly with God is given unusual tact and insight in dealing with difficult people.
36. A certain but sure sense of gratitude engulfs a person who knows the hand of God is on him.
37. There is an acute awareness that the Spirit of God provides opportunities and insights otherwise not available.
38. These "bonuses from God," lend great delight and joy to a life lived for the Lord.
39. Amid even the most exalted spiritual experiences there ever lingers the possibility of lapsing into sin.
40. The world and its allurements are ever with God's people. It requires eternal vigilance to guard against the allurements of our society and culture.
41. Even the best of men can fall prey to some insidious weakness in their makeup.
42. The ongoing effect of a godly life has an impact far beyond our fondest imagination. It is the impress of a spirit that has been controlled by the Spirit of God. Like a pebble dropped in a quiet pond, its waves of influence extend to the extremity of its periphery.
43. God has ordained that no person live as an island to himself. Our actions extend across the ages.
44. Only what a man lets go, does God ever get.
45. Spiritual courage, under God's control, carries its own great contagion.
46. It is not enough merely to destroy in the name of the Lord. He expects that something more noble and enduring shall be erected in its place.
47. A man under the control of God's Spirit is a formidable force for good in the world.

48. Few are the true peacemakers who may be highly honored with the title, "Child of God."
49. God's people do not deign to add insult to injury. Their words are weighed in honesty and sincerity.
50. The supreme secret to a serene walk with God lies in immediate obedience to His directives.

The life of Gideon, a simple countryman, comes down to us across the centuries undiminished in impact. He was a man who gave himself to God. In turn God has given him back to us for example, encouragement, and splendid inspiration.